CONNECTING WITH OLDER ADULTS:

Educational Responses and Approaches

The Professional Practices in Adult Education and Human Resource Development Series explores issues and concerns of practitioners who work in the broad range of settings in adult and continuing education and human resource development.

The books are intended to provide information and strategies on how to make practice more effective for professionals and those they serve. They are written from a practical viewpoint and provide a forum for instructors, administrators, policy makers, counselors, trainers, managers, program and organizational developers, instructional designers, and other related professionals.

Editorial correspondence should be sent to the Editor-in-Chief:

Michael W. Galbraith
Florida Atlantic University
Department of Educational Leadership
College of Education
Boca Raton, FL 33431

CONNECTING WITH OLDER ADULTS

Educational Responses and Approaches

Paulette T. Beatty
Texas A&M University
College Station, Texas

Mary Alice Wolf
Saint Joseph College
West Hartford, Connecticut

KRIEGER PUBLISHING COMPANY
MALABAR, FLORIDA
1996

Original Edition 1996

Printed and Published by
KRIEGER PUBLISHING COMPANY
KRIEGER DRIVE
MALABAR, FLORIDA 32950

Library of Congress Cataloging-In-Publication Data

Beatty, Paulette T., 1937–
Connecting with older adults : educational responses and approaches / Paulette T. Beatty, Mary Alice Wolf. — Original ed.
p. cm. — (Professional practices in adult education and human resource development series)
Includes bibliographical references and index.
ISBN 0-89464-752-0
1. Aged—Education—United States. 2. Adult education—United States. 3. Adult learning—United States. 4. Aging—United States. 5. Gerontology—United States. 6. Aged—United States—Social conditions. I. Wolf, Mary Alice. II. Title. III. Series.
LC5471.B43 1996
374′.973—dc20 95-3088
CIP

10 9 8 7 6 5 4 3 2

CONTENTS

PART III.

ENTERING THE WORLD OF PRACTICE

PART IV.

JOURNEY INTO THE FUTURE

PREFACE

Welcome to our aging society! Imagine, in 1990, persons over the age of 65 made up 16% of America's adult population and cast 22% of the votes in the 1990 elections (U.S. Bureau of the Census, 1992). In 1994, an estimated 31 million persons in this country were over 65, constituting 12% of the total U.S. population (U.S. Department of Health and Human Services, February, 1994); these figures represent the highest proportion of this age group in our nation's history (National Center for Health Statistics, 1994). In the year 2030, this group will comprise 21.1% of the total population. This demographic shift will dramatically alter our collective experience.

WHO SHOULD READ THE BOOK?

This book is for anyone who has thought about aging. What happens when I age? What can I do to age well? How can I help clients, relatives, neighbors, and friends as they, too, grow old?

This book is intended for beginners, a label which in some respects denotes all of us. Although we are all aging and have known and worked with older adults, we have not necessarily studied the process; nor have we had the opportunity to learn in a systematic and purposeful manner effective approaches for expanding the potential for personal growth, development, and learning which resides within all older adults. This book will serve as a guide for those who seek to enhance the full development of this population in ways that support independence and dignity.

This book is about learning. We expect it to help a wide array of professionals in higher education. For the generalist adult educator in training, it can supplement the knowledge base. It should prove helpful as a basic or complementary resource for students enrolled in programs or courses dealing with gerontology, social work, pastoral ministry, allied health, recreation and leisure, geriatrics, management, marketing, contemporary family, human service and education, human development through the life span, and counseling.

In addition, the information should meet the needs of professionals, paraprofessionals, and lay volunteers who wish to connect with older adults; it should benefit caregivers, family members, friends, and acquaintances. Others likely to find the book useful include adult educators, staff development directors, personnel managers, volunteer directors, community organizers, pastoral outreach workers, home companions to the elderly, nurses in diverse settings, dietitians, physicians, a whole range of persons in the social support networks of the elderly, and business persons who recognize the imperative of accommodating the needs and interests of their older clients or customers. Even elders themselves should gain from the reading.

Another cadre of should-be users of this publication is less obvious. This almost hidden component of the social support networks of older adults within the community includes firemen, postal workers, retail clerks, pharmacists, household and appliance repair crews, bank personnel, lawyers, family members, relatives, church or synagogue leaders, community volunteers, bill collectors, and neighbors. We hope that in these pages, readers will find their caregiving values reinforced, knowledge and insight expanded, response choices multiplied, and creativity turned loose in the service of our elders.

WHAT DOES THE BOOK CONTAIN?

This book addresses issues of aging, expectations for aged persons, and the means to respond in practical and educationally sound ways to the changing needs of older adults.

Part I, The Journey, contains one chapter, A Brave New World. As an introduction to the world of the older adult of today and tomorrow, it presents the major issues involving our older population and sets the stage for a practical engagement and connection with the aging in society.

Part II, Foundations for Practice, deals with the fields of gerontology, in Principles of Aging (Chapter 2), and adult education, in Principles of Learning (Chapter 3). Both chapters present major concepts and incorporate recent findings about aging and learning during adulthood. Each chapter lists significant principles derived from the disciplines of gerontology and adult education, which can be applied in various settings and situations. Worksheets and case studies are included to facilitate the reader's understanding of the principles. Chapter 4, Twelve Principles Integrated, consolidates the principles concerning aging and learning during adulthood so that they are useful for practitioners who wish to develop connections with a wide variety of older persons through educational outreach.

Part III, Entering the World of Practice, focuses on specific challenges that aging provides to the practitioner and builds upon the knowledge base presented in Part II. Chapter 5, Making Connections Happen, presents challenges faced by professionals, practitioners, friends, and family members as they make meaningful connections with older adults. In maximizing the application of the principles to their own settings, readers will analyze alternative responses, including dealing with older adults as individuals, as cohorts, or as members of the larger community.

Chapter 6, Vignettes with Reflections, introduces the life stories of older adults, representing a continuum of aging from the totally well and autonomous older adult, to the older adult in need of some assistance, to the frail elder requiring substantial intervention. The vignettes reflect the diversity of our older population in terms of gender, age, race and ethnicity, socioeconomic status, health, and kind of community. Readers will apply to the vignettes principles from the fields of gerontology and adult education in addressing major issues facing older adults such as education, leisure, spirituality, health, social welfare, family and social networks, community interaction, employment, and the aging community itself.

Part IV, Journey into the Future, contains Chapter 7, Challenges for the Future, which integrates the principles from both foundational disciplines and the applications presented earlier. This chapter presents major recommendations and identifies hallmarks of success in connecting with older adults. It challenges all helping persons to become members of "caring teams," networking for increased effectiveness. Finally, it invites readers into a dialogue about their experiences with older adults.

WHY WAS THE BOOK WRITTEN?

Many professionals, paraprofessionals, and lay volunteers who serve older adults lack knowledge about gerontology and adult education. In a practical manner, this publication blends these two arenas of professional practice.

HOW SHOULD THE BOOK BE USED?

This book uses principles from gerontology and adult education. It is organized from a need-to-know, practice-oriented perspective. If you are a novice in your experiences with older adults and are for the first time being challenged to recognize the new developmental patterns of older friends and family members, start at the very beginning to achieve a broad perspective of the worlds of gerontology and adult education. If you require information about the normal aging processes of aging, refer to Chapter 2, Principles of Aging. If you need to know more about learning in older adulthood, review the information in Chapter 3, Principles of Learning. If you recognize that an older client needs more assistance than you are prepared to provide, study the vignettes about frail elders in Chapter 6, Vignettes with Reflections.

This publication can be used as a handy reference, textbook, or a practice manual by people studying alone or in groups. The worksheets found at the end of the chapters and case studies are excellent devices for training and workshop presentations.

We envision this book as the first of two, the second being a compendium of success stories of hundreds of helping persons throughout the country. It will share the experiences of our readers who have made the principles of aging and learning work for them and their elders. It will be your book! We encourage you to share your stories with us as you make connections with the older adults in your lives. Welcome to our aging society.

ACKNOWLEDGMENTS

Many people helped with this work.

Mary Alice Wolf thanks the following persons who read early drafts and contributed to the content and shape of the final work: Barbara Atkins, Marsha Balet, Ann Dellert, Mary Jane Eisen, Joanne Grabinski, Susan Kline, Mary Estelle Minehan, Heidi Moore, Lucile Nahemow, Judith Picknelly, Helen M. Raisz, and Tony Wolf. She is grateful to Saint Joseph College for its support and caring environment, and particularly to the entire class of HDGE 560 "Older Adult as Learner" (Fall, 1992), and HDGE 593 "Educational Gerontology," (Fall, 1993). She dedicates this book to Tony Wolf, her husband, for being the best collaborator and partner and inspiring her development.

Paulette Beatty acknowledges Texas A&M University and the Association of Former Students for providing resources and time to engage in a faculty development leave while engaging in this work. She also thanks Jane Stallings and Lloyd Korhonen for their constant support in this undertaking. She dedicates this book to Kathryn and William Beatty, her parents, for being the best of mentors and friends and supporting all her undertakings.

THE AUTHORS

Paulette T. Beatty is a professor in the Educational Human Resource Development Department at Texas A&M University in College Station, Texas. Her national leadership initiatives include numerous publications in the field of adult education, membership on the Board of Directors of the American Association for Adult and Continuing Education, serving as Program Chair for the Association's national conference, and editorship of a research-to-practice journal, *Lifelong Learning*.

Dr. Beatty's professional specialty is in educational gerontology. In addition, her professional expertise is in instructional methodology; program development, including needs assessment and evaluation; group dynamics; and leadership and staff development.

Dr. Beatty received her Ph.D. in adult education from Florida State University in Tallahassee, Florida. She received her B.A. and M.S. degrees in biology from The College of Saint Rose in Albany, New York.

Mary Alice Wolf is associate professor of human development and gerontology and director of The Institute in Gerontology at Saint Joseph College, West Hartford, Connecticut. Her activities have included service on advisory boards in higher education, long-term care, community outreach in aging, and health and adult learning centers. She has conducted workshops in reminiscence and retirement and has served as retirement consultant to religious communities. She is the cofounder of The Consortium for Gerontological Education in Long-term Care, and has most recently developed and edited a curriculum for education of home companions to the elderly called *Gerontology for Companions.*

She has presented research findings at the Gerontological Society of America, the American Association for Adult and Continuing Education, National Council on the Aging, and Association for Gerontology in Higher Education. She is the author of *Older Adults: Learning in the Third Age*, a review and an annotated bibliography of literature about the older learner for ERIC, the Clearinghouse on Adult, Career, and Vocational Education; currently she is working on an edited collection of essays on learning about aging through women's literature.

Dr. Wolf holds an Ed.D. from the University of Massachusetts, an M.A. from Columbia University, a Certificate from the Sorbonne, University of Paris, and a B.A. in English from Boston University.

Part I

The Journey

Part I, The Journey, welcomes the reader to the world of our aging population, and highlights the major demographic shifts taking place today. It introduces the challenges faced by all members of society as they strive to better integrate the increasingly significant constituency of older adults. It presents a kaleidoscope of issues central to the quality of life and life satisfaction of older adults both in contemporary and future societies. It sets the stage for all readers to reflect as they confront their own aging and interact in the lives of older adults.

CHAPTER 1

A Brave New World

THE SOCIETAL SHIFT

We are aging. When the first census was taken in 1790, only 2% of the population was 65 years of age or older; by 1980, older adults comprised 11.3% of the entire population; and by 2030, an expected 21.1% of the population will be members of the older generation. There are currently 31 million Americans over the age of 65. Changing demographics within the population as a whole and within the older population have been attributed to advances in medicine, increased education, emerging wellness movements, changes in social mores, and individual lifestyle choices. These changes inevitably impact all members of our heterogeneous society and will continue to influence relationships among its members. The following section presents some of the characteristics of the current population of older adults: demographics, family connections, spiritual and physical lifestyle, and work characteristics.

Demographic Characteristics of Older Americans

The composition of the older population itself is changing because of increased longevity. The forty years between 1960 and 2000 have seen a significant shift within the population of older adults: the young-old (65–74), middle-old (75–84), and old-old (85 and over). By the year 2000, the young-old will decrease from 66.2% to 50.5% of the older population; the middle-old will increase from 27.7% to 34.9% and the percentage of old-old will shift from 6% to 14.7%. According to mortality rates, women continue to outlive men within all racial and ethnic groups (U.S. Department of Health and Human Services, February, 1994). Consequently, the death of a spouse is predominantly a female experience.

Other characteristics of the aging society are notable. Persons 65 and older report fewer acute conditions per person per year than other age groups; however, they report a higher number of days when activities are restricted. Further, over 85% of those 65 years of age and older experience one or more chronic conditions; and of those reporting these conditions, approximately 46% have some limitation of activity attributable to the condition.

For the middle-old and older population as a whole, 66.6% of the women compared with 2.6% of the men are widowed, a pattern which is fairly consistent among white, black, and Hispanic elderly. The educational levels are rising, most notably among the young-old of all racial and ethnic groups, although there are variations among these groups (U.S. Department of Health and Human Services, May 1994).

Economic self-sufficiency for the older population is improving, at least as measured by the poverty rate, which fell from 35.2% in 1959 to 14.1% in 1983. The picture varies greatly, however, depending upon gender and race or ethnicity. White males predictably experienced the lowest poverty rate among older adults, 8.2%; and black females had the highest poverty rate, 41.7% in 1983. Approximately 95% are living in typical community households as opposed to nursing homes or other homes for the aged. Geographic mobility, though typically understood as the prerogative of young and middle adulthood, is also a phenomenon with the older adult population. Although the magnitude of such moves, especially in and out of states, is relatively small, they do occur—usually because of decisions to retire or move closer to younger family members. Our older population is indeed heterogeneous (Atchley, 1994; U.S. Department of Health and Human Services, May 1994).

Older adults face many challenges during this stage of

their lives, all of which call for adaptations in behavior in order for the experience of aging to be productive.

BONDING AND SOCIAL CONNECTEDNESS

A great diversity exists in what constitutes family for older adults in our society. The family of an older adult might consist of a spouse, adult children, grandchildren, siblings, a parent, a mother or father in-law, and an array of distant kin. Whatever its configuration, older adults typically turn first to family in time of need.

The family unit constitutes the primary buffer and support for members as they face life's challenges. The bonds within a family can meet intimacy and affection needs and provide a sense of belonging. Yet these bonds, so important in primary relationships, are fragile and must be nurtured if they are to serve all members of the family well. A graphic illustration of the frailty of these bonds is the disproportionate increase of divorce among the older population. The increase in the divorce rate is expected to continue.

Many older adults are living longer, independently and at some distance from family members, on a restricted income, and with one or more chronic conditions. Given these new realities, some functions may no longer be fulfilled by families. Instead, nonfamily members in the older adult's informal or formal network will be called upon to meet fundamental needs.

Caregiving for older family members, or friends and associates, has only recently emerged as a developmental task of middle age. It places additional strain upon members of this "sandwich" generation who are typically not prepared to manage the demands of caregiving. The need for care takes many forms as the fabric of life changes for older adults: financial assistance, emotional support, physical assistance in the daily activities of living, and decision-making assistance in such areas as health, housing, and transportation. Knowledge of the dynamics, demands, and implications of caregiving is the caregiver's best asset (Springer & Brubaker, 1984).

THE HUMAN SPIRIT

When one considers the human spirit, two perspectives are particularly worthy of attention: religion and spirituality. First, many older adults have explicitly religious concerns associated with organized religious bodies. Here it is important to address how they are ministered to and supported within the religious groups with which they are affiliated, how they are provided with opportunities to contribute within the local congregational community and, last, how they are integrated into the fabric of the life of the local congregation. One's faith community has helped to shape one's belief system and has often been a steady and trusted resource in facing life's challenges. Thus it contributes significantly to one's overall definition of self.

Often older adults have opportunities, desires, and needs to interact with pastoral caregivers who are trained, committed, and therefore capable of assisting them to meet important challenges: rabbis, ministers, priests, doctors and staff in hospitals and nursing homes, as well as directors of religious education or adult spirituality in congregational settings. These persons constitute the primary professional vanguard as issues of personal identity, spirituality, meaning making, hope, and despair are addressed. Others in the ever-changing social networks of older adults can also be instrumental in making positive connections with older adults: counselors, psychologists, physicians, nurses, employers, employers, educators, and social workers. Also fulfilling key roles in the lives of aging individuals are members of their informal support network: family, relatives, and friends.

PHYSICAL WELL-BEING

Invite young or middle-aged adults to fantasize about what their lives will be like at 60 or 70 or 80 or 90 years of age. See

Worksheet 1.1 at the end of this chapter to begin the process of thinking about aging. Rarely will they mention the physical limitations, chronic or acute conditions, which will inevitably impact their overall quality of life. Invite older adults in their 60s, 70s, 80s, or 90s to talk about their experience and daily activities as older adults, and you will hear a markedly different story.

The reality is that the normal aging process is accompanied by some physical limitations. Other factors influencing physical well-being and life expectancy are the environment in which one lives, one's ethnicity and gender, and lifestyle choices made over decades. The development and progression of cardiovascular disease and cancer, today's two leading causes of death, have been associated, at least in some degree, with individual health behaviors (Cavanaugh, 1993).

Initiatives to promote wellness are common today in a variety of settings. They can be found in work sites since a healthy work force, both young and old, positively impacts the bottom line for business and industry. Hospitals and clinics, health spas, recreation departments, and school systems are among the most likely providers. Wellness programs are also found in community centers, in both for-profit and nonprofit agencies. They introduce participants to a wide range of behaviors that support a healthy lifestyle such as stress management, appropriate exercise, balanced nutrition, smoking cessation, and alcohol moderation. Ultimately, all behaviors supporting a healthy lifestyle must be deliberately integrated into one's way of life.

LIFESTYLE CHOICES, WORK, AND LEISURE

Topics addressed in workshops on retirement planning typically include lifestyle planning; financial planning; wellness and healthcare planning; interpersonal and social network review; housing, living arrangements and relocation explorations; and leisure time and work option review (The National Council on the Aging, 1991). Decisions made about retirement are greatly affected by adequate financial resources and physical health. If these two resources are available, then viable choices among alternatives exist; otherwise, options are severely curtailed.

It is never too early to start planning for old age. Economic self-sufficiency ensures that older adults have viable choices in terms of housing, relocation, transportation, coverage for medical necessities, food, clothing, and money for discretionary purposes. Americans are often shocked to find that they will spend nearly a third of their lives in retirement and that opportunities for self-development and generativity must be created.

Recent studies have indicated that even when retirement is possible from an economic perspective, many older adults find meaning in paid work. The needs to be socially active, to belong, and to contribute are frequently cited as reasons either to remain in the work force or reenter it after a period of retirement (AARP, 1987). Studies have revealed that employers now recognize the advantages of retaining older workers. Their loyalty, dependability, and expert knowledge are characteristics in short supply. Given the age shift in the U.S. population, we can expect to encounter fewer and fewer qualified workers entering the work force in the years ahead; hence, the necessity to develop those qualified employees already in place (Hale, 1990; Shea, 1991).

The journey of aging is a dramatic and challenging one, touching on every area of human experience. What roles can we play? How can we be prepared for more and more older adults whose contributions, needs, and development can be integrated into a wide array of activities? What educational strategies and approaches will best respond to this demographic shift? How can we provide outreach to those older adults who may require some assistance to fully participate in society? The following chapters address these issues and explore ways in which all of us can connect with older adults.

WORKSHEET 1.1

What are some of the ways you would complete these phrases? List here some definitions that come to mind:

> Older people are. . . .
>
> Men over 80 are. . . .
>
> Women in their 70's are. . . .
>
> Sex and older adults. . . .

1. Take five minutes to explore your responses.
2. If you are working with a class or group, break into groups of four to discuss the responses. When the group comes together again, ask for some common responses to the trigger phrases.
3. What responses have you had that relate to this area?
4. What educational responses might you suggest in working with this area?

Part II

Foundations for Practice

Part II, Foundations for Practice, introduces the reader to two sets of principles: six principles of aging (Chapter 2) and six principles of learning (Chapter 3). To work with older persons, we must understand how development takes place throughout the lifespan. Our purposes are to explore the issues important to older adults and to introduce the foundations of adult learning which enhance our work as helpers, creating environments and learning opportunities for professionals, neighbors, educators, and older persons themselves. Through probing questions, stimulus activities, case studies, and application worksheets, the reader is provided with opportunities to reflect upon these principles. In Chapter 4, these two sets of principles are integrated into a single set appropriate for the processes of aging and learning. Thus Part II provides the foundation to facilitate work with older adults.

CHAPTER 2

Principles of Aging

This chapter provides an overview of gerontology, the study of aging. Six principles of aging are presented in detail, providing a framework for our understanding of older persons. Each principle is discussed, supported by aging research, and further refined through a variety of worksheets. The principles are:

1. Aging is a developmental process.
2. Each older adult is unique.
3. Older adults should maximize physiological and psychological capacities.
4. Locus of control is a central issue throughout life.
5. Continuity of self is lifelong.
6. Older adults need to be meaningfully connected.

PRINCIPLE ONE: AGING IS A DEVELOPMENTAL PROCESS

To appreciate aging as a developmental process requires a change in attitude because, in Western culture, aging is typically regarded as a physiological phenomenon. We joke about turning 40 and often label older people in negative ways. We focus on the physiological changes that occur as we age. But the truth is that many older people continue to live healthy, autono-

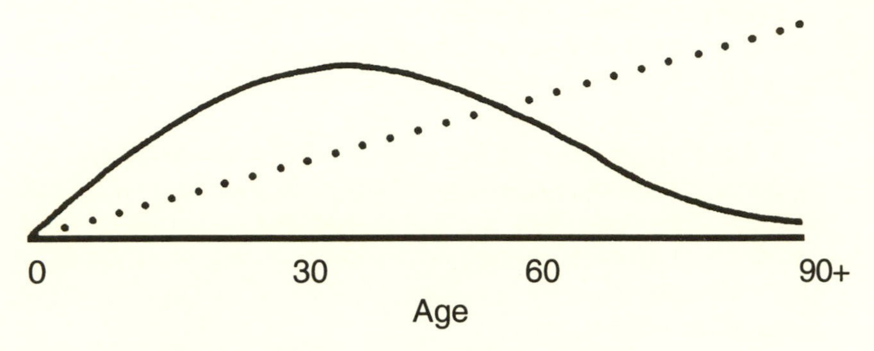

Figure 2.1 A Developmentalist's Perception of Biological Growth Contrasting with Psychosocial and Spiritual Growth

mous lives. Gerontologists have recently begun to study the lives of older adults who are "successfully aging" (Rowe, 1987; Rowe & Kahn, 1987).

A model of developmental growth shows that human beings actually evolve during the entire lifespan. This developmental model, the authors' own, demonstrates the disparity between a vision of life in which biology is the centerpiece and a vision of life in which the total personality is the focal point. To understand aging from a developmental perspective, picture a graph marking how we all grow. The curved line traces the biological version of age. The straight line follows the developmental perspective. In the biological model, the peak of development is at age 30; in the psychosocial model, the individual grows and gains in integration, experience, wisdom, and other human qualities with aging. Figure 2.1 presents this view.

In normal aging, there are no drastic changes which occur at a certain age. No one suddenly grows old. Everything is part of a process which commences at birth or conception and ends at death. These changes unfold as we mature, and life is an ongoing event of maturing.

Ask any 30–50 year old when middle age starts, and the typical response is that it is not imminent. Indeed, middle age is a life stage that others are arriving at, but we ourselves have not quite reached. Although, as Erma Bombeck says, we were all in the same high school class, you have aged, but I, through some miracle, have not.

To examine your own attitudes about aging and your own development, complete Worksheet 2.1 at the end of this chapter, and share the results with someone you know.

Erik Erikson's (1963, 1982) model is most useful to our understanding of development and aging. He described lifelong growth as related to tasks which must be performed. At each stage of life, times of stability are followed by developmental crises. Upon resolving the crisis, the individual can enjoy the particular beauty and security of that psychosocial stage and go on to the next. The stages are cyclical and predictable: alternating periods of crisis, stagnation, and growth. We can grow to fullness with age.

Table 2.1 presents an abbreviated overview of Erikson's eight-stage model of development (Erikson, 1963). Through the model we understand that aging is truly a developmental process. While it is true that every life follows a unique path, there are many similarities which we observe between our lives and the lives of others. The similarities have been noted by those developmentalists who seek to describe the paths that most people follow through life.

Throughout life we continuously develop and renew ourselves, and the world looks different to us from each new van-

Table 2.1 Erik Erikson's Eight Stages of Development

Stage	Label	Development Challenge
1	Basic Trust vs. Mistrust	The task is to feel safe, comfortable, and to trust. This stage occurs in the first months of infancy and is a foundation for all subsequent stages.
2	Automony vs. Shame and Doubt	Having achieved a sense of security and belonging, the child begins to explore the world. The child experiments, feeling confident in moving away from the parent's reach and out into the interesting world.
3	Initiative vs. Guilt	The child now enjoys trying things further exploring the boundaries of the immediate world. There is a spirit of adventure. However, the skills and sense of independence, the "moving out into the world" are successful because of the parental connection and the trust established within.
4	Industry vs. Inferiority	Now in school, the child "learns to win recognition by producing things." At this stage, one continues to trust in one's own abilities and begins to see oneself as worker, student, teammate, friend.
5	Identity vs. Role Confusion	The youngster, now in adolescence, seeks a personal "self." Some identity develops in terms of work and future plans. This is a time of experimentation and boundary-testing.
6	Intimacy vs. Isolation	Having achieved a sense of self, the young adult looks for a partner or a group with which to merge. Trust, again, is central to the successful mastery of this task.
7	Generativity vs. Stagnation	Adult now, the individual seeks to create a family, to produce goods and make meaningful contributions to the welfare of others. This stage lasts all of adulthood.
8	Ego Integrity vs. Despair	This last stage is "the harvest" of all the other stages. In old age the individual comes to terms with "oneness," and has a sense of the order of the world.

Adapted from E. Erikson. (1963). *Childhood and Society* (2nd ed.). New York: W. W. Norton.

tage point. Each of us can recall an "Aha!" experience when suddenly we have had a new awareness of reality. Robert Kegan (1982) called this an "emerging reality." We see, for example, that our parents are just human beings who tried to do their best, not the ogres we thought they were when we were teenagers. Or we see that a job, although satisfying in many ways, is not all there is to life. Sometimes these awarenesses or developmental moments are brought on by a crisis—the death of a parent or spouse, the loss of a home through catastrophe—and sometimes they quietly evolve. As we age and mature, we see things differently. It is not what we see that has changed, but ourselves.

By the time one is old, one has seen many changes; one has amassed many memories. Most individuals have experienced losses—a job, a friend, a spouse, a child, a home—and have had to reconstruct a life after a loss. They have also experienced successes and accomplishments—a loving spouse, children, career achievements, financial success, a good reputation; these individuals have developed a new sense of themselves with each positive experience. Both successes and losses can touch life at any age. They generate memories of youthful dances, hungry children, hunger, love, and separation. Recent studies have shown that retrieving memories of past struggles and successes is beneficial to health and well-being (Birren & Deutchman, 1991; Butler, 1982b; Kaminsky, 1984; Wolf, 1990). Elders have new stages, new ways of integrating their experiences into a meaningful whole, and new insights.

As helping professionals, how can we best participate in this developmental process as people age? Consider the following approaches to connect with an elder's world and to help elders integrate their lives.

Reminiscence Activities

Encourage reminiscence. This process often helps the task of integration. It helped Mae Reynolds, age 82, who seemed to rediscover her girlhood after the death of her husband of 60 years. No one in the family knew about her life before marriage. She talked about her first job in a factory. As a child laborer, she had to hide in a barrel every time the supervisor came through the mill. But when she was only 13, she sent a hundred dollars home to her family. How vivid are her stories now that she has time to reminisce!

Learning Opportunities

Provide learning for new integration. Opportunities for spiritual growth are as welcome in old age as at any other time in our lives. Tim Orlando was strangely touched by the music at a recent funeral of an acquaintance. The music brought back a flood of childhood memories. An agnostic all his adult life, Tim found himself weeping at religious invocations. A new world had been opened to him. This was not, he said, a throwback to a former childhood faith, but a new kind of appreciation for his undeveloped spiritual side. Now interested in learning about liturgical music, he has enrolled in a course at a local community college.

Meaningful Time

Allow elders to spend time in ways that are meaningful to them, rather than in busy tasks. Bernice Neugarten and associates (1968) have written eloquently of the process of "greater interiority" in later adulthood. She found that, starting in midlife, individuals become increasingly concerned with "time left to live rather than time since birth" (Neugarten & Datan, 1974). Time is regarded as valuable, and activities must be deemed worthwhile. Thus, activities no longer considered important are discontinued. Note that older adults are not "disengaging," as some have theorized, but merely recentering.

Contrary to the stereotype that elders are neglected and

isolated, older adults frequently visit with their families and friends. They do make choices based on their individual situations and inclinations. In understanding the "needs" of older persons, we must learn to ask them what they want, rather than design activities and interventions for them based on what *we* think they want or what we imagine is appropriate for elder individuals.

PRINCIPLE TWO: EACH OLDER ADULT IS UNIQUE

Often we lump mature adults together, labeling them all as "old." Yet a woman of 72 may be "younger" than a man of 59. She may be healthier, more vital, more flexible, and may be a practicing lawyer who has never had a major illness. The gentleman at 59 may be a cardiac risk and have no teeth. Recognizing differences in aging is extremely important for all helping persons and especially so for policy makers, planners, and gerontologists who typically categorize older adults as "young-old" (65 to 74), "old" (75 to 84), and "old-old" (85 or over). Bernice Neugarten, to whom this categorization is attributed, now suggests that these distinctions have been misnamed and misunderstood (Neugarten & Neugarten, 1986; Neugarten, 1990). Aging, she believes, should be regarded in terms of need, health, and wellness, and not chronology alone.

Several myths about the aged must be unlearned, for they are only half truths at best, unfounded and inappropriately generalized to a broad array of persons. One myth is that older adults end their lives in nursing homes. In fact, at any one time, only 5% of persons over the age of 65 are in long-term care settings (Maddox, 1987). Another myth is that all older persons are unhappy. Indeed, surveys of older adults regularly dispel this myth. A third myth is that all older people are alike. The typical gerontological response is, "How could they be? They have had more time to become different from each other than any other age group!" Each older adult is unique, possessing a unique story and set of capacities to meet life's challenges. Worksheet 2.2 helps the reader explore this principle.

PRINCIPLE THREE: OLDER ADULTS SHOULD MAXIMIZE PHYSIOLOGICAL AND PSYCHOLOGICAL CAPACITIES

As caring helpers, we should understand the normal body and intellectual changes that occur in aging. This section presents an overview of that process.

What happens in aging? Of course, each of us ages differently. We begin to see in middle age the changes associated with older adulthood. Some changes are visible, others are not. While there are certain standard physical characteristics of aging, each of us will fulfill our own genetic and environmental mandate. Our physical conditioning will also play a pivotal role. For example, a nonsmoking, physically fit woman well into her 70s may have no diseases. Her sister, who has led a sedentary life, is overweight, and smokes, may develop heart or lung problems. If diabetes is a family trait, neither woman may exhibit signs of diabetes or one or both may show signs of the disease. Conditions caused by alcoholism, malnutrition, continued stress, and overmedication can damage the older person's health. The ensuing decline is related to physical well-being and not to aging per se. There is great individual variability in the aging process.

Recently, Rowe and Kahn (1987) have reported on research done over the past 30 years that differentiates the normal processes of the maturing body, which we have come to understand as "successful aging," from the specific diseases which sometimes accompany aging. By studying healthy older adults who are community residents, researchers have tried to discover guidelines that "would not be contaminated with changes related to specific disease processes" (Rowe & Kahn, 1987, p. 1). The aim is to examine what happens in "normal" as opposed to "successful" aging. In the normal physiology of aging, a number of general changes can be observed.

The Senses

All five senses show decline with age: vision, hearing, taste, touch, and smell. Those working with adults over 65, should adjust the environment accordingly. Good light, low speaking tones, and elimination of auditory distractions such as the buzz of an air conditioner will contribute to good communication. Because older persons' acuity of taste, touch, and smell decline, families or caregivers should monitor daily living conditions of frail elders who could be oversalting food, burning themselves while cooking, or failing to smell smoke during a household emergency. Fortunately, assisting devices such as hearing aids and eyeglasses combined with accommodations to the environment can lessen the impact of several of these sensory losses.

Body Composition

Older people actually become shorter. This is due, in part, to a stiffening of the elastic cushioning of the vertebrae. The disease of osteoporosis, twice as common in women as men, involves continued loss of bone mass and increased brittleness. Small hairline fractures occur and persons with osteoporosis may fall, causing further bone damage. In this country, the elderly suffer over one million fractures annually (Rowe & Kahn, 1987). By conducting a safety check of the older adults' living spaces, helpers can remove hazards and reduce the chance of falls or other accidents. Adequate nutrition can also lessen the impact of body changes.

Cognitive Functioning

Contrary to assumptions, recent research findings (Schaie & Willis, 1986; Schaie, Willis, Hertzog & Schulenberg, 1987) show that older persons may not decline in cognitive functioning. Older persons who keep active and stimulated may actually raise their scores on intelligence tests. Research is beginning to focus upon the multiple dimensions of intelligence and to explore approaches to measuring intelligence that are much more appropriate to a mature constituency. Memory training, too, can assist those experiencing episodic memory loss.

The Muscular System

Muscles become stiff with age, losing elasticity and strength. It is important for older persons to continue using muscular capacity, especially to regain movement after illness or injury. A loss of strength can be reversed in individuals who exercise (Deobil, 1989; Goldberg & Hagberg, 1990).

The Digestive System

Many changes associated with aging are actually attributable to lifestyle, poor nutrition, lack of exercise, and medications (Ausman & Russell, 1990). When nutrition is adjusted and adequate exercise occurs, many problems can be corrected. Although loss of taste buds and slower digestive processes do in fact call for accommodations, new approaches can be learned.

Homeostasis

With aging, the body responds differently; homeostasis is the ability to adapt physically. This homeostatic change may affect energy level, body temperature, sleep habits, metabolic function, and the efficiency of the immune system. Adapting to these changes rather than fighting them can enable one to retain a good and satisfying quality of life.

The Nervous System

With aging, reaction time slows, affecting the way one plays games, drives, and responds to questions. When older adults who have retired from the work force decide to return, they often fear that they can no longer complete the same tasks as quickly as they did as younger workers. But in fact, older persons may function better at certain tasks. A former assembly line worker, for example, may excel as a receptionist where the skills required are friendliness and patience (Atchley, 1987; Bass, 1993; Butler & Gleason, 1985).

Skin Changes

Typical are the wrinkles and age spots we associate with the elderly; in persons who have not been in the sun, these changes are less likely to occur. Other noticeable marks of aging include loss of hair, graying of the hair, decrease in sweating, and increased dry skin (Perlmutter & Hall, 1992; Spence, 1989). Beauty, in our society, is defined as young, lean, and agile. As helpers, we need to remind mature persons that there is in fact more than one standard, and that they too have a beauty —both physically and psychologically.

Sleep Patterns

Older people tend to sleep fewer hours than younger persons. At age 25, the average night's sleep is 7 hours; at 60, 6 hours; at 75, 5 hours (Atchley, 1994). In addition, older adults may awaken several times during the night. They can, however, learn strategies to obtain adequate sleep to meet the demands of daily living.

Causes of Death

The leading causes of death in older persons today are heart disease, cancer, and cerebrovascular disease. Environmental features such as nutrition, exercise, psychological factors, and social settings affect these conditions. Increasingly, research indicates that our lifelong environment and lifestyle choices play a significant role in ameliorating conditions associated with the aging body.

As we learn more about the normal physical and cognitive changes that occur in aging, we realize that the "use it or lose it" adage is indeed valid.

Use Worksheet 2.3 to explore the changes discussed in physical and cognitive functioning.

PRINCIPLE FOUR: LOCUS OF CONTROL IS A CENTRAL ISSUE THROUGHOUT LIFE

The concept of locus (place) of control (or autonomy), which can be internal or external, refers to decision making throughout our lifespan. From our earliest moments in life, when we depend on others for our well-being, we develop through a process of separating and attaching. (See Table 2.1 for Erikson's model.) We begin to organize our demands for food and comfort through this interactive means, and we acquire control over our environment (Mahler, 1976; Stern, 1985). Babies explore their ability to curb their impulses (Kegan, 1982); gradually, young children begin to make demands on the environment. Life is a continuous process of organizing this phenomenon.

As we mature, we find that others depend on us and we depend on others. Yet we have an ongoing drive to be autonomous, to take control of as many decisions in our life as possible. This drive exists even when we choose to be dependent on someone else, to join a group, to be a member of a family. From the 2-year-old's earliest "No! Me do it!" to the 92-year-old's "No, thank you, I'd rather do it myself," we wish to be in charge. This is the "internal" locus of control. The "external" locus of control refers to instances when we must succumb to the wishes of others, when an outside force is, appropriately or inappropriately, making a decision for us.

The "fear of loss of control over one's environment is often mentioned by the elderly" (Feingold & Werby, 1990, p. 25). Research shows that when institutionalized elders are given a role in decision making, they respond with physical and psychological improvement and a greater feeling of wellness (Feingold & Werby, 1990; Langer & Rodin, 1977; Rodin, 1986; Rodin & Langer, 1977). Worksheet 2.4 explores this concept.

PRINCIPLE FIVE: CONTINUITY OF SELF IS LIFELONG

Recently, an adult educator was working with a group of older adults who were planning a talent night. One couple offered to perform folk songs, play the guitar, and lead group singing activities. Once professional singers, they said they would drop off publicity literature. The next day a pile of glossy five-by-eight photographs of "The Singing Duet" appeared on the adult educator's desk. The photos showed an attractive couple in their twenties. "Are these Jane and Howard's children?" the educator asked her colleague. "No, that's Jane and Howard themselves," responded the colleague. "They said you needed some publicity material for talent night." The photographs did indeed resemble Jane and Howard, now in their seventies. Apparently, this was how Jane and Howard saw themselves. They were, after all, the very same people they had been years ago with the same talents—another example of continuity of self.

We develop a lifelong sense of ourselves that is connected and whole. We do not perceive ourselves as different during the aging process, we are just slightly older versions of ourselves, wrinkled but totally recognizable. All of us—although we certainly do grow and develop—are products of our own lives, our own experiences. Gerontological literature stresses the continuity of personality throughout the lifespan (Fiske & Chiriboga, 1990; McCrae & Costa, 1984; Neugarten, 1979). "Personality" is defined in *Webster's New Third International Dictionary* as "the totality of an individual's behavioral and emotional tendencies" (1963, p. 1687). Two psychologists who studied lifelong personal characteristics concluded, "Ask not how life's experiences change personality; ask instead how personality shapes lives" (McCrae & Costa, 1984, p. 3). Along this vein, in *Remembrance of Things Past*, Marcel Proust wrote:

> For man is a creature without any fixed age, who has the faculty of becoming, in a few seconds, many years younger, and who, surrounded by the walls of the time through which he has lived, floats within them but as though in a basin the surface level of which is constantly changing, so as to bring him into the range now of one epoch, now of another. (1981, p. 767)

Use the case study presented in Worksheet 2.5 to explore the principle that continuity of self is lifelong.

PRINCIPLE SIX: OLDER ADULTS NEED TO BE MEANINGFULLY CONNECTED

A fact of life is that we are all interdependent. Each of us needs to be a part of a community and to play a part in the world. As we grow older, we find that contributing to others is a means of connecting and of elevating our own self-concept. Erikson (1963, 1982), and subsequently his associates, (Erikson, Erikson & Kivnick, 1986) revealed that through adulthood there is a great need to be generative, to care for others, to work for the next generation. Erikson contends that we grow through generativity. If we do not grow, we may become hypochondriacs, self-absorbed and stagnant.

Practitioners who connect with older adults should provide outlets for the need to contribute. Educators have produced intergenerational curricula to involve older adults in the lives of younger people (Birren & Deutchman, 1991; McClusky, 1990; Moody, 1988, 1990; Wolf, 1992a). For example, training programs have been developed to help older persons to become politically active and to counsel their peers.

It is important to observe, however, that each person makes meaning in highly individual ways: what is important to you may not be important to your neighbor. If we are to connect with older adults, we need to understand how they find meaning and develop educational approaches to enhance this spirit of individual purpose and perspective. Older adults must be meaningfully connected. Worksheet 2.6 should help us to understand how to apply this principle.

SUMMARY

These six principles of aging articulate the developmental processes of the human being from birth to death: psychological, social, spiritual, environmental, and physical. To approach older adults, to make connections, and to respond to the multiple and rich possibilities of their later life, we must understand these principles of aging and how to apply them with sensitivity and care in interacting with older adults.

WORKSHEET 2.1

To explore the first principle of aging, "Aging is a developmental process," complete the following lifeline. Your birth year is at 0 on the lifeline. Enter your present age at the appropriate place on the lifeline. Enter your anticipated age at death at the appropriate place on the lifeline. Then, under the lifeline, list events from your life that you most vividly recall.

Your lifeline:

0___10___20___30___40___50___60___70___80___90___100

Review your lifeline and answer the following questions.

1. What occurred to you when you saw your place on the lifeline?
2. Did you notice any differences from the lifelines of others whom you know?
3. Did you notice any commonalities with the lifelines of others whom you know?
4. Did you note any times that you actually connected with others, even when it appeared that you were disconnecting?
5. Using the lifeline, how would you now describe your "development"?

Complete the following sentences.

1. Aging begins. . . . .
2. Middle age starts. . . .
3. You know you're old when . . .

Look at your responses and consider the following questions.

1. Are you surprised at your responses?
2. Are you becoming aware of any preconceptions you have about aging?

WORKSHEET 2.2

Imagine that you are a concerned neighbor of Agnes M. Apply the second principle to her situation. The second principle asserts that "Each older adult is unique."

Agnes M.

Agnes M., a 69-year-old widow, is generally in good health although she has experienced a loss of bone mass due to osteoporosis. Her interests are far ranging: travel, movies, dance classes, and volunteer activity at an inner-city elementary school. Her daughters, Edith and Marian, live nearby and try to engage Mrs. M. in their households. Edith, particularly, wishes Mrs. M. to attend Sunday dinner and to babysit for her three young sons.

Review this vignette and consider the following questions.

1. How would you describe Mrs. M?
2. Have you stereotyped her?
3. How would you begin to "help" Agnes M.?
4. How do you think that Agnes M. would describe her own situation?
5. How might Agnes M.'s description of herself differ from your description?
6. In what ways can the principle that "each older adult is unique" help you establish a connection with Agnes M.?

WORKSHEET 2.3

Complete this worksheet to explore the third principle of aging, "Older adults should maximize physiological and psychological capacities."

Identify three family members or acquaintances with the following age distributions: a young-old person (aged 55 to 65), a mid-old person (aged 65 to 75) and an old-old person (aged 75 and older). Engage each of these persons individually in a conversation and pose the following questions to each one.

1. What physical changes have taken place as you have aged?
2. Did these physical changes happen suddenly, or were they gradual?
3. Were you able to made satisfactory accommodations to these physical changes?
4. Do you think these changes are part of the process of normal, healthy aging or were they attributable to lifestyle choices or other environmental factors?
5. What concerns do you have about future *physical* changes as you continue to age?

Repeat these questions and ask about *psychological* changes instead of physical changes.

Repeat these questions and ask about *social* changes.

WORKSHEET 2.4

Review the following vignette with Principle Four in mind: "Locus of control is a central issue throughout life."

Matthew Angelo

Matthew Angelo is an 82-year-old retired mechanic in excellent health. He lives with his wife of 60 years, Edna. Their modest lifestyle accommodates the needs of Edna, who has heart disease. Mr. Angelo takes his wife to her medical appointments, to the supermarket, and to visit her nearby sister. However, on his last visit to his doctor, Mr. Angelo was told his eyesight had declined and his driver's license would not be renewed. Mr. Angelo was appalled: What would this mean to his lifestyle, to his wife, and to his self-esteem?

Review this vignette and consider the following questions.

1. What would you do to help Mr. Angelo keep his autonomy?
   a. If you are a neighbor
   b. If you are an outreach worker at the local senior center or parish
   c. If you are a relative
   d. If you are a nurse in the physician's office
   e. If you are his physician
   f. If you are his wife
2. How would you handle these concerns?
   a. Locus of control
   b. Gender sensitivity
   c. Continuity of self
   d. Interdependence
   e. Privacy
3. How could this problem affect the relationship between Mr. Angelo and his wife? Be aware that Mr. A's cohort is especially pained when asking for help. (Picture John Wayne asking for help.)
4. Is it appropriate for anyone to become involved if Mr. A. has not asked for help?

WORKSHEET 2.5

This worksheet presents a case study of Principle Five, "Continuity of self is lifelong."

Dr. Benjamin Granneck was on duty in the emergency room of Springfield Hospital recently. An elderly woman had been brought in who appeared to be senile, confused. "You know, Doc," said the police officer, "mental—like they get at that age. Poor lady."

"Indeed, the woman, Miss Louise B., was rambling incoherently," recalls Dr. Granneck. " 'I'm lost,' she kept saying, 'I know I parked behind the dry cleaning store I always go to. Now I can't seem to find my car.' "

Many qualified neurologists might have asked Miss B. the classic questions from the Mental Status Questionnaire (MSQ) and declared her incompetent when she couldn't answer what day it was or who was president. (Usually these MSQ questions are: 1. What is the name of this place? 2. Where is it? 3. What is today's date? 4. Month? 5. Year? 6. How old are you? (within two years) 7. When were you born? (Month) 8. When were you born? (Year) 9. Who is the president of the United States? 10. Who was president before him?)

Yet Dr. Granneck simply observed, "Oh, that Louise B! She was always like that! Even in grammar school. A garrulous and confused dingbat!" As it happens, our Miss B. was an age-cohort of Dr. Granneck's; they had gone to elementary and secondary school together. They exchanged greetings and, after a few moments of calming conversation, he assessed the problem. Miss B.'s car had been towed. She had indeed parked behind the dry cleaning store and now, without having kept her hairdresser's appointment and without eating lunch, she was somewhat lost and incoherent. She was given a snack and driven home.

"What a silly girl she was in the old days," recalled Dr. Granneck. "She certainly hasn't changed a bit." Dr. Granneck—himself nearly seventy—then returned to his work. Within his workplace, where he wears an air of confidence and competence, no one would have labeled him senile. Rather, he looked the part of an elder physician, the old family "Doc."

This case study warns about stereotyping of older adults; we often label them senile just because they appear confused in certain circumstances. Such labels are unfair. Each elder is the integration of a lifetime of experience, growth and development, and his/her unique personality. With age, one's identity becomes more pronounced.

Review the case study and consider the following questions.

1. Have you ever been stereotyped?
2. If so, what characteristic caused the person to stereotype you: age, race, ethnicity, gender, educational level, socioeconomic status, language, physical appearance, or a physical or psychological disability?
3. What conversation would you like to have had with the person who stereotyped you?
4. What approaches would you suggest to someone who has been stereotyped because of age?

WORKSHEET 2.6

This worksheet presents a case study based on Principle Six, "Older adults need to be meaningfully connected."

Claudette R. is a 79-year-old retired school teacher. She has been a volunteer, with a small stipend, at Colonial Village (a museum) for fourteen years, joining the staff the same day she retired from her school job. Never married, Miss R. has used the job site for social and financial gain. She is paid a small salary to sit in an eighteenth century home. She wears the antique outfit of a preacher's wife and explains the customs of eighteenth century America to thousands of visitors each year. Her coworkers adore her and she has been a surrogate grandmother to dozens of young workers who have passed through the village.

Recently, however, Miss R. has changed. She frequently arrives late at the parsonage, is often disheveled, and does not bathe regularly. She appears lost, asks questions to which she once knew the answers, and is confused. The staff of Colonial Village has rallied around Miss R., protecting her from the director's notice and covering for her at training sessions and at her post in the parsonage. Since this is clearly not a temporary problem, Miss R.'s coworkers are alarmed. They need to know what they should do.

Review the case study and consider the following questions.

1. What transitions are being experienced by Miss R.?
2. What level of connectedness is Miss R. currently experiencing?
3. Who should be involved in responding to this situation?
4. What are the implications of intervening in Miss R.'s situation?
5. Which of the six principles can you apply to this case study?
    a. Aging is a developmental process.
    b. Each older adult is unique.
    c. Older adults should maximize physiological and psychological capacities.
    d. Locus of control is a central issue throughout life.
    e. Continuity of self is lifelong.
    f. Older adults need to be meaningfully connected.
6. How would you, as a coworker, help Miss R. in this time of transition?

CHAPTER 3

Principles of Learning

This chapter presents six principles that provide the basis for an informed engagement in the challenges of learning for older adults themselves and for all of us who wish to relate to older adults as family members, friends, service providers, and caring professionals. These principles can guide us in connecting with older persons and facilitating their learning in ways that enhance personal development. Through a series of individual guided activities, each principle is presented and further explored:

1. Learning is a process involving multiple personal changes.
2. Individual needs, emotions, and approaches to learning shape the learning experience.
3. Learning capacity is adequate for meeting life challenges.
4. The learner actively constructs the future.
5. Life experience is the foundation and resource for all learning.
6. Personal and social contexts affect learning.

PRINCIPLE ONE: LEARNING IS A PROCESS INVOLVING MULTIPLE PERSONAL CHANGES

Structured activities and experiences designed to achieve specific learning outcomes are often referred to as adult education. Adult education happens in many settings, usually through gatherings, in order to ensure a functional society with fully contributing and fully actualized members. There are driving classes, consumer education workshops, peer counseling training courses, and on-the-job training, to name but a few of the undertakings which we recognize as adult education. Adult education also encompasses the independent, self-directed purposeful pursuit of learning. We may set out to master the automatic teller machine, the fine points of watercoloring, the psalms of the Bible, or a full range of consumer skills. In fact, however, when we think of all of the educational experiences we have had, whether independent or collective undertakings, we will have accounted for only a small fragment of the total reservoir of what we have learned throughout life.

There is more to learning however, than simply the structured experiences noted above. Adult learning is the ubiquitous and sometimes mysterious process of personal change which enables us to adapt to the demands of our environment, shape that environment, and realize personal potential. There are many contexts within which learning occurs, and there are many types of change which we call learning. Learning can be incidental to the process of living; it can happen as an intended result of specific activities. Typically, it takes place with our full consciousness; at other times, learning seems to be so imperceptible that " . . . some events occurring at the periphery of experience and awareness are somehow internalized" (Jarvis, 1992, p. 11). For example, we are quite aware when we have finally mastered a half dozen or so idiomatic expressions in Spanish which we wanted to use in conversation with our new Spanish-speaking friends. On the other hand, we may surprise even ourselves when we suddenly realize that we have made the transition from the stage of intense grieving over the loss of a spouse and have assumed the role of mentor for several recently widowed friends.

We must lay aside the conventional wisdom that adult education and adult learning are the same thing, so that we can recognize that learning is as normal as breathing and that it permeates the totality of our lives.

But what is learning? Many definitions have been developed and many theories have been offered to explain the phenomenon of learning. Currently, no single approach or perspective appears capable of providing a comprehensive explanation of the diverse manifestations of personal learning throughout the life span. Each limited perspective is, however, useful in contributing to our understanding. Each offers "different assumptions about learning and . . . helpful insights into adult learning" (Merriam & Caffarella, 1991, p. 125.) Five distinct perspectives will be briefly introduced: behavioral, cognitive, social, humanistic, and critical.

The Behaviorist Tradition

For proponents of the behaviorist tradition, namely Thorndike (1931) and Skinner (1968), learning is simply a change in one's behavior. There is relatively little concern about intrapsychic processes which may accompany the change. Behaviorists explain learning in the following manner. A desired response, learning, or change in behavior, is produced by an external stimulus. New behaviors are incorporated into one's behavioral pattern if and when they are associated with pleasurable effects; continued practice under positive circumstances will consolidate the learned behavior; and when an individual is in a position of readiness, learning will take place. Further, if actions are rewarded or reinforced, they will tend to recur; while those that are not reinforced will soon disappear.

Although the modification of behavior may appear highly manipulative, it has been used effectively in programs promoting health-related lifestyle changes in such areas as diet, exercise, smoking cessation, and stress reduction. The challenge is to determine what would constitute a reward for the individual seeking a change of behavior, how to ensure continued practice of the behavior, and how to appropriately reinforce the behavior. The challenge facing helping persons is to assist older adults to become more adept at shaping their own environment to effect these desired behavioral changes.

The Cognitivist Tradition

From the cognitivist perspective, learning is explained and takes place principally through intrapsychic processes. Once this has been said, it is important to note that the principal proponents make differing contributions to our understanding of what learning is and how it takes place. Bruner (1973) describes learning as the process of discovery where the learner must place each new experience in meaningful relationship with other like experiences. No one else can do this for the learner, although others can facilitate the process. Since all learners have different experiential backgrounds, they will learn different things, assign different meanings to what has been learned, and then solve problems in novel situations from their unique perspectives. Personal and active engagement in the process of change is at the heart of learning. Ausubel (1968) concurs that meaningful learning must be related to what is already part of the individual's knowledge or understanding. However, he is concerned that the process of discovery is too error-prone for many kinds of learning. Consequently, the organization and categorization of new information and its relation to prior knowledge needs to be provided for the learner. This structure should set the stage for the new learning as well as facilitate the transfer of learning from one type of task to another. The notion of a hierarchy in learning tasks has been contributed by Gagne (1970). Accordingly, all learning must proceed from simpler tasks to more complex tasks. Complex learning is achieved through incremental attainment of small learning tasks.

The cognitivist tradition has much to offer us. How many times learners shy away from a new learning challenge because it seems beyond their ability, whereas a hierarchy of learning tasks could reduce that challenge. How many times help in the organization and structuring of a learning task pays off handsomely! How many times we have been caught in delight by a wonderful "aha" experience when we have been encouraged to discover, problem solve, and experience some capacity which we did not recognize we possessed.

The Social Learning Orientation

Albert Bandura (1977, 1986) consistently integrates both the behaviorists' and cognitivists' explanations of the phenomenon of learning. While he roundly rejects the notion that all learning is necessarily reflected in behavior and that all learning is the product of stimuli external to the individual, he readily acknowledges that both behavioral change and external stimuli provide appropriate and adequate explanations for some types of learning. On the other hand, he recognizes the importance of changes in intrapsychic processes, and he asserts that self-determination plays a role in the process of learning, especially at the higher levels.

According to Bandura, we make judgments as individuals about how well we can deal with prospective situations perceived as challenging, ambiguous, unpredictable, or stressful. These judgments—our assessment of self-efficacy—are major determinants of whether we venture forth into the uncertain world, whether we dare to learn. We base these judgments upon information derived from, personal accomplishments, observations or other vicarious experiences, various types of social influence including verbal persuasion, and physical arousal. These multiple and interacting sources of information are powerful shapers of the persons we both view ourselves to be and the persons we are willing to become.

The Humanistic Perspective

Humanists focus not upon behavioral change or cognitive processing but rather upon the totality of the person: mind, perceptions, emotions, values, motivations, and aspirations. Maslow's "hierarchy of needs" (1970) illustrates how the satisfaction of specific needs beginning at the lower levels on the hierarchy paves the way to satisfaction of higher level needs; first survival needs, then safety needs, then belonging needs, and finally self-esteem needs serve as the motivators for all human undertakings in the ultimate quest for self-actualization at the pinnacle of the hierarchy. Learning is ultimately directed toward the goal of self-actualization.

Rogers describes that type of learning which leads to personal growth and development in his works on client-centered therapy (1983). It is characterized by total personal involvement, personal discovery, pervasive shaping of the individual learner, self-monitoring and evaluation of the process, and a focus on the meaningfulness of the experience. For those who wish to help others, Rogers offers several fundamental tenets of learner-centered teaching. Individuals are responsible for their own learning; we can only help facilitate the process. Individuals actively embrace learning which helps to the maintain or enhance their sense of self. Individuals resist experiences which can cause a change in self-perception. An individual's sense of self under perceived threat becomes more rigid and relaxes only when one is completely free from threat. Significant learning is promoted when threat is reduced and when individuals are assisted in relating to the environment in nondefensive and constructive ways (Knowles, 1973, pp. 32–33).

In sum, humanists offer a view of learning which totally engages and shapes the individual and is central to the personal sense of who one is and who one is becoming.

The Critical View

The critical perspective, an explanation of certain types of learning, contends that "knowledge cannot be taught but must be constructed by the learner" (Candy, 1991, p. 252), and that learning represents "a qualitative transformation of understanding rather than a quantitative accretion. . . . " (Candy, 1991, p. 249).

Proponents call for the critical scrutiny of " . . . values, beliefs, and assumptions . . . [frequently] uncritically assimilated from the dominant culture" in an effort to make meaningful our life experience and to take important steps toward personal growth and development (Brookfield, 1989, p. 205). This process of learning requires us to identify and challenge our assumptions, reflect on the importance of context, imagine and explore alternatives, and allow for reflective skepticism (Brookfield, 1987). Transformational learning involves changes in consciousness and worldview. This process of perspective transformation is triggered by a defining and/or destabilizing experience, and is followed by self-examination, critical assessment of assumptions, recognition that one's experience is not totally unique, exploration of options for the future, planning for the future, acquisition of needed knowledge and skill, tentative venture into the desired future, development and maturation into the path that was chosen, and reintegration into the new reality (Mezirow, 1991).

As helpers, we must understand the role which transformative and critical learning plays in all of our lives. This learning totally engages individuals and inevitably results in personal changes of significant proportions.

In sum, there are multiple types of learning, not just one type. Each new behavior enacted, each new skill acquired, each new bit of information gained or problem solved, each new attitude consolidated on the path to personal development, each new social role mastered, each new "aha" experience, each new reframing of our personal life experience—all these together contribute to the construction of the "forever becoming" person. Learners themselves can be assisted to take charge of these processes of personal change and become better able to learn. Learning, then, is not merely "education" or "schooling," but the ongoing process of personal change with multiple manifestations.

To explore the first principle, that "Learning is a process involving multiple personal changes," complete Worksheet 3.1 at the end of this chapter.

PRINCIPLE TWO: INDIVIDUAL NEEDS, EMOTIONS, AND APPROACHES TO LEARNING SHAPE THE LEARNING EXPERIENCE

Even though we understand the commonality of our experiences as learners, we must recognize that our learning experiences have unique dimensions that define them as truly our own. This uniqueness stems from three characteristics; namely, our particular needs, our emotional frame of reference, and our approaches to the challenge of learning. Thus, when we become truly helping persons, we succeed in our attempts to meet individual needs, to recognize the emotions which are embedded in the learning experience of each individual, and to employ strategies which capitalize upon individual approaches to learning.

Needs as Driving Forces for Learning

Howard McClusky (1974) asserted that older adults had five types of needs related to the challenge of learning: coping, contributing, influencing, expressing, and transcending. Over the course of a lifetime, these needs would emerge, be met, and re-emerge in different configurations. Learning engages the total person in a continuous process of growth and development, often initiated by the daily challenges of life.

McClusky provided us with a functional framework for five fundamental questions regarding human needs. What are the challenges for coping on a day-to-day basis that engage our older adult in lifelong learning? Might they include living on a restricted budget, managing arthritic pain, or getting a good night's sleep? What are the challenges for those who long to contribute in a meaningful way during the postretirement or empty-nest years? Might they include learning to find new ways to practice the skills that have been developed over a lifetime; making a part-time retirement career choice; or contributing to political, social, economic, and religious goals? What are the challenges for those who have a need to influence the course of life around them? Might they include finding new ways to affect the values of their grandchildren, shaping corporate responsiveness to a mature clientele, publicizing views in the political arena, or volunteering for peer counseling training provided by the local agency on aging? What are the challenges for those who have a need to express that which is a source of gratification and joy? Might they include involvement with poetry, artistic expression, singing, or photography; crafting activities such as sewing, cooking, woodworking, or gardening; taking up adventure sports; or other creative endeavors? What are the challenges for those who need to place in context the meaning of life, to transcend the immediate? Might they include reading or viewing the great pieces of literature or drama; placing belief in God; or working through the loss caused by separation or death? All of these challenges represent opportunities which all of us can embrace and so continue to shape our future.

Emotions as Accompaniments to Learning

Learning is not solely an undertaking that engages an otherwise idle brain. Learning is a matter of the heart as well. When we are challenged to change and to learn, we are challenged as whole persons. It is a mistake to think of learning as an emotion-free undertaking. There are "paradoxes" (Jarvis, 1992) which are linked to the process of learning itself. These include self-concept and self-esteem, stability and change, unlearning and learning, the known and the unknown, practical and theoretical knowledge, and control and submission. An exploration of these paradoxes provides an understanding of the emotional character conceivably present within all learning experiences, including formal and nonformal experiences, daily experiences and self-directed undertakings.

Self-Concept and Self-Esteem

One's self-concept and self-esteem are important elements in undertaking new learning experiences. If we do not believe in our ability to succeed (self-concept), then, regardless of the learning agenda, we will feel negative about ourselves (self-esteem) and will refrain from, withdraw from, or become dysfunctional in such experiences. Yet, insofar as all learning beckons us to become more than we presently are, it calls for a realistic assessment of where we need to change. Thus, in order to engage in effective learning we must continually redefine ourselves and change the values and feelings attached to our definitions. For example, one might enter a defensive driving class with a firm belief that one is a safe driver after many years without an accident or citation; the reason for being there may be simply to achieve a deduction in auto insurance premiums. During the first session, one may be surprised by new safe driving practices introduced. Suddenly one may feel more tentative about oneself as a safe driver, less confident and proud.

Stability and Change

The process of our human condition is best described as intermittent stability and change. Change can be unnerving, and we generally strive for periods of stability in our lives. Yet, learning requires that we develop new skills, ways of viewing ourselves or others, patterns of thinking, or range of behaviors. Naturally, it takes time before these new behaviors, beliefs, values, or perspectives will be fully integrated into our lives. Once change has been integrated into our lives, we enter a new period of stability. Take, for example, the pattern of relationships that has developed over many years when one member of a couple was employed full-time. A stable preretirement pattern became ingrained. Now, retirement dawns. A new pattern of relationships must be established in order to accommodate the needs and interests of both persons. This process of change can be difficult, yet accommodations are necessary in order to establish new patterns of stability with which both persons can live in some degree of comfort. Ideally these patterns will support growth for both members.

Unlearning and Learning

When a task requires that a set of behaviors be replaced, we speak of unlearning before relearning. Lewin (1947) explains the process of change as that of requiring something or someone to unfreeze from the current state, move to the new state, and then refreeze. Unlearning causes one to give up what has become part of a personal repertoire in order to build a new repertoire. This is not easily done, and it is generally an emotional-laden process. Consider a volunteer enrolled in the hospice volunteer training program. One of the basic tenets of hospice is that the personal values, traditions, and wishes of the terminally ill patient and the members of the family are to be honored. The volunteer is to be as supportive of the wishes of the family as possible and as unobtrusive in the family environment as is compatible with providing the assistance needed. Suppose a volunteer who has totally different personal standards of order and cleanliness, and who wishes to provide religious support different from what is desired. Some unlearning must take place in order for the volunteer to truly serve the needs of the host family.

The Known and The Unknown

The dilemma facing persons willing to engage in learning is to move from the known to the unknown. Suppose, for example, that the local branch bank serving a community has recently closed down and currently provides only an automatic teller machine (ATM) at that site. Customers who do not wish to travel the distance to the main bank must venture into the unknown. Previously, they knew all they needed to know to conduct their banking business. Now, they are not sure what to do at the ATM even though they have received a PIN and a set of written instructions in the mail. A number of approaches are possible: have a trusted friend handle the banking, go to the ATM with a knowledgeable companion, ask a bank employee to demonstrate, learn independently by trial and error, or bank by mail.

Practical and Theoretical Knowledge

Much of our practical knowledge, our wisdom, derives from our daily experiences through which we have learned. Often, unfortunately, this practical knowledge is discounted.

Nevertheless, when one has successfully arbitrated a dispute between two preschoolers, one's reputation soars. One immediately becomes a font of wisdom for the young parents and wisdom has received its true recognition.

Control and Submission

Is not much of the experience of maturing into adulthood related to becoming increasingly autonomous and gradually leaving dependencies behind? Our ability to exercise appropriate control within our lives is important to our self-concept and our self-esteem. Yet, in many instances calling for change in our lives, we must temporarily share control with others; we must trust others to act in our best interests. For example, Charlie X has just undergone heart surgery; his cardiologist has placed him on a regimen of exercise, no smoking, moderate drinking, and a new diet. Yet Charlie has always been afraid of "over-exercising," believing it could do more harm than good. Further, his chest x-rays don't show any visible damage from his long-standing smoking habit. He reluctantly accepts the idea that he should drink less and modify his diet. In this case, Charlie X must comply with the recommendations in order to maximize the chances for recovery. He must suspend his beliefs both in the danger of exercise and in the benign character of his smoking habit. He must make consistent efforts in all facets of the therapeutic program. None of these changes will be physically or emotionally easy.

Preferred Approaches as Shapers of Learning

Part of our uniqueness in learning relates to our preferred and typical approaches to learning. "Each individual has preferred ways of organizing all that he sees and remembers and thinks about. Consistent individual differences in these ways of organizing and processing information have come to be called cognitive styles" (Messick, 1976, pp 4–5). At least nineteen different styles have been identified and studied. For example, we may prefer social interaction in learning rather than independence; or we may prefer to read, or observe, or try out new skills and behaviors. We may prefer to see the whole picture before getting specific information; we may wish to take few risks or many in our learning activities; we may differ in our tendency to categorize, focus attention, or scan a broader field. These are only a few of the many ways in which we can expect to differ from others in facing change experiences.

Indeed, it is remarkable to observe that individual needs, emotions, and approaches to learning shape learning experience. As helpers, we must recognize that we have within our grasp the tools to foster change by responding to people as individuals (see Worksheet 3.2).

PRINCIPLE THREE: LEARNING CAPACITY IS ADEQUATE FOR MEETING LIFE CHALLENGES

Learning is a lifelong capacity for personal change, and the individual can adapt to meet life's challenges. Too often we hear the saying, "You can't teach an old dog new tricks." Frequently, such sayings have incorrectly and unnecessarily become the scripts and the self-fulfilling prophecies of avowed nonlearners. However, important conclusions about one's continued capacity to learn emerge from a study of intelligence, cognitive development, memory, creativity, and wisdom.

Intelligence

It is typically assumed that intelligence is a single capacity measurable by tests. Yet this notion is not only limiting but also fallacious (Cattell, 1963; Guilford, 1967; Gardner, 1983; Sternberg, 1990). Cattell proposes two types of intelligence: one (fluid) associated with primary biological and/or neurological functioning, and another (crystallized) associated with life experience and education. While capacities dependent upon fluid intelligence can be expected to peak and wane during our lives, capacities dependent upon crystallized intelligence continue to develop across the life span. Guilford explains intelligence as the interplay among what is to be learned, the mental process involved in learning, and the learning outcome itself. Intelligence is manifest when these three dimensions appropriately mesh. Gardner identifies seven types of intelligence: language, logic and mathematics, spatial, music, movement, self-understanding, understanding of others. Finally, Sternberg claims that intelligence involves not only applying cognitive processes, but also utilizing life experience, and engaging in socially sensitive and appropriate behaviors. In sum, intelligence takes multiple forms and life experience contributes significantly to intelligence.

Cognitive Development

The process of cognitive development continues into adulthood. Researchers use the terms relativistic and dialectical to characterize adult capacities to think (Merriam & Caffarella, 1991). The ability to deal with ambiguity, take circumstances into account when forming judgments, and view things as neither totally right nor totally wrong are characteristic of the maturation and development of cognitive abilities during adulthood. For example, one may strongly oppose divorce. Yet, when a family's savings may be depleted through catastrophic illness of one spouse, the alternative of divorce as a means of protecting family assets may appear reasonable.

Memory

Even though "loss of memory" is often associated with old age, the facts do not support this contention. Memory is now understood to have four stages. In the first stage of processing incoming information from the environment (sensory memory), a great deal of information is retained for a brief period. With age may come a slowness in the speed of handling incoming information, making whatever is not processed at this stage subsequently unavailable. Then, information which has passed through sensory memory is available to be processed later (working or primary memory); at this stage memory capacity is small, but primary memory is longer lived than sensory memory. Memory losses associated with this stage are linked to a decreased capacity to use strategies for organizing and rehearsing information. In the third stage, the ability to recall the routine of our daily lives (secondary memory), may show some decline with age primarily because strategies for organizing and retrieving information have not been employed. Memory of the distant past (tertiary or long-term memory) appears to be relatively unaffected by age (Cavanaugh, 1993).

Consequently, we conclude that statements on the inevitability of memory loss and its accompanying debilitating effects are oversimplifications of a complex process.

Creativity

Creativity has been studied by a number of researchers, and different definitions and measures of creativity have yielded different results. It has been aptly noted that, "If we cannot decide how to measure creativity, then it will be difficult to determine how to optimize it (Stevens-Long, 1984, p. 425). Further, it is suggested that different stages of creativity manifest themselves over the life cycle: spontaneous expression, technical proficiency and skills, inventiveness or ingenuity, innovative building upon or reconfiguration of ideas, and pure originality. Some discussions of creativity focus upon divergent thinking analogous to problem-solving, and point to its presence throughout the lifespan (Kimmel, 1990).

Wisdom

Wisdom, the ability to apply knowledge to the experience of living, is often considered the pinnacle of adult thinking.

"Wisdom is in some way the store of knowledge, opinions, and insights gained, often through long years of life" (Jarvis, 1992, p. 202). The truly wise, regardless of age, are able to see in totally new situations or contexts what has been learned through past relevant life experiences. The wise see a unity in life and understand when apparent differences in situations are, in fact, superficial. Wisdom is spoken of as expert knowledge about the fundamental issues of life (Cavanaugh, 1993) and is noted through its hallmarks: a practical expertise, an ability to define and solve problems, a recognition of the differences in problems at various developmental stages, an understanding of values as the basis upon which ethical and moral decisions are made, and a clear sense of the demands which life problems present (Baltes, 1993; Dittmann-Kohli & Baltes, 1990).

In essence, a new understanding of adult intelligence supports belief in the ongoing capacity for learning throughout the lifespan. We recognize that any age-related decreases in memory as well as in response speed can be ameliorated. We recognize that throughout life we are capable of different forms of cognitive development and creativity. Last, we recognize the possibility that with increased age comes experience and the potential of growth in wisdom. Indeed, learning capacity is adequate for meeting lifelong challenges. Worksheet 3.3 gives us a chance to review this principle.

PRINCIPLE FOUR: THE LEARNER ACTIVELY CONSTRUCTS THE FUTURE

The responsibility for learning rests primarily within the individual. Whether we identify forces intrinsic or extrinsic to the individual as providing the stimulus for personal change, the choice is made by the individual for or against growth and development. One can choose to embrace or resist change.

The choice to embrace change can manifest itself in actions such as these: to consciously buckle one's seat belt, to learn to prepare healthy foods, to develop effective peer counselor skills, to undertake the care of grandchildren, to assert rights and concerns as a consumer, to initiate contacts for accessing senior services, to develop a new senior outreach ministry among the local churches, to write memoirs, to become a member of the Silver Haired Legislature, to gather information about retirement communities, to learn how to increase the security of one's home or apartment.

Since most learning happens in everyday contexts, learners must of necessity take charge of their own learning, a process which requires the development of a certain level of personal autonomy. Referred to as self-directed learning, autonomy in functioning is held by many as a universal purpose of adult education.

Tough (1971) studied "adult learning projects"; that is, learning activities of at least seven hours duration initiated by individuals during which time they actively pursued a specific learning agenda. Later, in a related stream of research, Tough (1982) explored the phenomenon of intentional change, again initiated by individuals. Tough discussed with his respondents the processes involved in each type of venture and found a great proliferation of episodes in which adults were taking charge of their own learning and their own change processes. Aslanian and Brickell (1980) in *Americans in Transition* have noted that change in life events triggers engagement in learning for adults. Certainly, the lives of older adults are replete with transitions. Consequently, one can anticipate that learning might well be embraced by this population as a means of coping and adapting to changing circumstances.

In the most definitive work to date, *Self-Direction for Lifelong Learning*, Candy (1991) offers suggestions to foster autonomy within the learner. The goal is to "encourage self-direction" and ultimately to "involve the learners in acting autonomously." Suggestions include: making use of learners' existing knowledge, encouraging deep-level learning, increasing question-asking by learners, developing critical thinking, enhancing reading skills, improving comprehension monitoring, and creating a supportive climate for learning (Candy, 1991, p. 322). Using the literature of adult education, Candy provides a profile of the autonomous learner including 134 "attributes, characteristics, qualities, and competencies" clustered into 13 groupings. The learner capable of autonomous learning will characteristically: be methodical and disciplined; be logical and analytical; be reflective and self-aware; demonstrate curiosity, openness, and motivation; be flexible; be independent and interpersonally competent; be persistent and responsible; be venturesome and creative; show confidence and have a positive self-concept; be independent and self-sufficient; have developed information-seeking and retrieval skills; have knowledge about and skill at learning; and develop and use criteria for evaluating (Candy, 1991, 459–466).

We now see that the responsibility for learning must rest within the individual learner who actively constructs the future and that we as facilitators can foster personal autonomy (see Worksheet 3.4).

PRINCIPLE FIVE: LIFE EXPERIENCE IS THE FOUNDATION AND RESOURCE FOR ALL LEARNING

During a taped conversation with Bill Moyers in the early eighties, Myles Horton, a radical educator in the tradition of Paulo Freire, observed that we only learn from the experiences that we learn from. Our experiences are the foundation for all learning; in order to apply our experiences to our new situation, we must analyze them.

Experiences can lead to destructive behavioral patterns, erroneous information, dysfunctional patterns of thinking, and negative or biased attitudes—all of which hinder personal effectiveness and interpersonal competence. People told repeatedly in youth that they can not learn will, without further critical reflection and without subsequent opportunity to disprove the assertion, inevitably reduce their reach for learning. In these instances, the patterns must be unfrozen before change and "refreezing" of new patterns can take place. It is important to undertake this process because life experiences are the foundation and resource for learning.

On the other hand, it is equally true that many of our experiences have positioned us to embrace opportunities for new learning. We may have learned correct carriage and good posture in grade school, or we may have learned about the elements of pairs dancing from a dancing school. Both of these experiences may help us as we learn new stretching exercises or selected line dancing steps. We may have learned respect for the rights of others within the family unit. This attribute may be one of the most important building blocks when we accept a volunteer position as nursing home ombudsman.

In efforts to foster individual change, we must find those life experiences, positive or negative, which are relevant to the task at hand. How critical it is, therefore, as friends, relatives, and helpers, to learn the biographies of older adults and to assist them to recall their biographies, refocus them, and apply them to new challenges of learning. Use Worksheet 3.5 to reinforce conclusions about the role of life experience as the foundation and resource for all learning.

PRINCIPLE SIX: PERSONAL AND SOCIAL CONTEXTS AFFECT LEARNING

Recent studies raise questions about the impact of one's personal and social context upon the experience of learning. First, how is learning shaped by our personal position within society, our family values and beliefs, and our social roles and responsibilities as individuals and citizens? Second, how is learning shaped by the society in which we live, its unique period in history, and its values and cultural norms?

The very fiber of our personal world shapes how we approach learning and how we embrace new opportunities for change. The roles and responsibilities which we assume at different periods shape our personal learning agendas. Our transitions between and among roles and responsibilities become, according to Havighurst (1972), the "teachable moments" when there is a unique readiness for learning which can truly enable us to grow beyond our current selves. Equally strong shapers are the values regarding education and learning which we share with other members of our nuclear and extended families; our educational and socioeconomic backgrounds; and our capacity to engage in formal, nonformal, informal and self-directed learning activities.

The society in which we live during the final decade of the twentieth century colors everything about learning during later adulthood. Who would have thought even 20 years ago that retirees would be reentering the workforce in record numbers, that they would be learning to utilize the latest technological tools, or that they would be taking exercise classes? Who would have thought that grandparents would be learning to care for a newborn crack-cocaine grandchild born to a drug addicted mother? Who would have thought that the political map of the world would have changed so radically in recent years that the U.S.S.R. no longer exists, that there is no divided Germany? New challenges abound as members of our society struggle to keep abreast of changes in the geopolitical landscape. Adults are now learning of the choices which are theirs as they face life-threatening health problems. "Advanced directives" and "medical power of attorney" are concepts working their way into the lives of all members of still rapidly changing society.

Indeed, the final principle of learning, that personal and social contexts affect learning, is most essential to our discussion of connecting with older adults (see Worksheet 3.6).

SUMMARY

The chapter on adult learning has focused on the literature and research of adult education. Its six principles contribute to our making meaningful connections with older adults by providing approaches and responses that help all people grow. Chapter Four provides the integration of the principles of adult learning and the principles of aging to help people better fulfill their roles as helpers of older adults.

WORKSHEET 3.1

This worksheet explores the first principle, that "Learning is a process involving multiple personal changes."

If you think back over the past year or two, you may be surprised at how much you have changed, grown, and learned. First, pick a specific date a year or so ago, and keep that date in mind. Then, complete the following items as you believe you would have done so on the date you selected. Next, complete the same items expressing how you feel now.

The best part of being who I am right now is . . .

One of my greatest assets is . . .

When I face a new challenge, I . . .

The most important person in my life is . . .

I get my strength from . . .

What I enjoy doing most is . . .

I'm really proud of myself because . . .

My greatest concern is . . .

I'd like to be able to influence . . .

I'd like to be asked to . . .

I wish I were more like . . .

I think I should . . .

I don't know how I would get along without . . .

I'm glad I learned . . .

I'm glad I am able to . . .

I'm glad I know how to . . .

I don't understand . . .

Family and friends think that I am . . .

Family and friends think that I should . . .

Overall, I feel I am . . .

How did you describe yourself a year ago? How did you describe yourself now? Are there differences in how you have described yourself at these two points in time? Focus upon the items in which you responded differently. What experiences may have caused these changes? Which of these experiences resulted in new learning for you? Were they formal educational activities which you undertook, or were they events that occurred in the process of daily living? What exactly did you learn and how did you change?

WORKSHEET 3.2

According to the second principle, "Individual needs, emotions, and approaches to learning shape the learning experience."

Let's think about the uniqueness of each individual as he or she faces an opportunity for growth and development. Select one of the following two activities for engaging in this principle.

1. ACTIVITY ONE:

A local congregation is initiating a series of daytime workshops called "Effective Grandparents: What Every Child Desperately Needs." Organizers hope that mature members of the congregation will enroll in the workshops and agree to serve as surrogate grandparents for the couples with children in the congregation as well as for the Big Brother and Big Sister organizations in the community. Twenty persons have signed up for the workshops. Let us take a glimpse into the lives of just six of the members of the congregation who have signed up as workshop participants.

> June is a gregarious 72-year-old, who has been widowed for almost a year. Her own grandchildren are themselves young adults and she misses the opportunity to help influence the children during their very formative years. June is confident that she has learned a great deal through raising her own children and interacting with her grandchildren. She prides herself in having read many of the books published on child rearing. She is looking forward to the opportunity to learn new approaches and have some "warm and cuddly" times again.
>
> Tom and Margaret are a couple in their mid-sixties. They have both just retired from lifelong careers in the local community where they worked as sales clerks in a major retail outlet. They always felt that they missed a great deal since they never had children of their own, nor did they choose to adopt children. Now is a wonderful time when they can start grandparenting.
>
> Tanya is a single professional woman in her late sixties who recently retired. Her MBA catapulted her into one career advancement after another and life has been very full for her.

Since her retirement she has devoted a great deal of time as a volunteer to local political causes and as a hospice volunteer. She wants to "give back" for having received so much. She is not sure how fully she as a single woman will be welcomed into the grandparenting program.

Ralph and Lisa are both in their mid-fifties. They have three children, all married and out on their own, and four grandchildren. Ralph works full time at the only job he has ever held, as a mailman. He is reasonably well off and has never permitted Lisa to work outside the house. They have just received a call from one of their daughters, who, after finalizing a bitter divorce, has been awarded full custody of her two preschool children. She successfully presented a case for her ex-husband's abuse of the children. Ralph and Lisa want to help their daughter and have told her to come home and to bring the children, no questions asked. Privately however, Ralph and Lisa feel that their tranquil lives are about to be turned into a living nightmare.

For each of these participants, answer the following questions:

1. What kinds of needs might they be bringing to the workshops?
2. What kinds of emotions might they be experiencing as they begin participation in the workshops?
3. What might their preferred approaches to learning be during the workshops?

Can you think of others who might be participants in the workshops? What might their stories be? What needs might they hope to have met through the workshops? What emotions might they feel as they engage in the workshops? What might be their preferred approaches to learning?

How could the facilitator help to meet the needs, address the emotions, and accommodate the preferred approaches of the participants?

2. ACTIVITY TWO:

Identify a new experience such as learning a sport or instrument, taking on a role or challenge, or coping with an unexpected problem.

1. What needs were you seeking to meet by engaging in this learning experience?
2. List the types of needs which were discussed.
3. What emotions did you experience as you undertook this learning experience?
4. What paradoxes accompany learning activities?
5. What preferred approaches were you probably applying in the learning activities?

WORKSHEET 3.3

Select one of the three activities appropriate for the third principle, "Learning capacity is adequate for meeting life challenges."

1. ACTIVITY ONE:

Identify an older person you admire. What is it about this person that you admire? Talk to this person, and discuss how he or she came to develop that attribute. Can this person identify specific occasions when this attribute was used as a personal resource in meeting new life challenges? How does this person feel that this attribute has contributed to overall success and life satisfaction? Can the information this person has shared with you serve as a model for you as you face your own life challenges?

2. ACTIVITY TWO:

Think about a personal attribute, asset, or skill about which you are proudest. How did you develop that attribute? How have you used this attribute in the past in meeting new challenges? How could you use it in the present and in the future as a personal resource? How has this attribute contributed to your overall success and life satisfaction?

3. ACTIVITY THREE:

Identify a challenging experience which you have faced in the not too distant past. What made this a challenging experience? What specifically did you do? What personal skills did you employ? What new skills did you need to develop in handling the experience? How successful do you think you were in managing that experience? Are you more prepared today to handle similar experiences? What can you do now to prepare yourself to address this type of challenge in the future?

WORKSHEET 3.4

This worksheet presents two activities, one with several variations from which to choose as you work to apply the fourth principle, "The learner actively constructs the future."

We are all Joe or Mary Bricks-and-Mortar. We are the building blocks of our own futures. We are also the master craftsmen in the work of our lifetime with multiple tools for the job of making the "we" of the future. This is exactly what we have been doing in constructing the persons that we are today. We have been building upon what we have already become.

1. ACTIVITY ONE:

First, label three sheets of paper "Goals, Tools, Actions." On the first sheet, list at least three of your specific goals for change and personal development. Choose those things which are distant aspirations, things from your wish list. Beside each goal list the reasons you wish to achieve it. Then, keeping the first sheet in plain view, list on the second sheet all the tools you have to use as you set out to achieve your goals and fashion the future you. This list of your assets may include values, knowledge, skills, social networks, material resources, time, enthusiasm, or health. Make this list as complete as possible, for it can be as valuable to you as money in the bank. Each time you use a tool in a new situation, work to improve the tools, or develop new ones, you are engaged in "personal asset management."

Finally, on the third sheet, identify those specific actions which you can take to employ your current assets (tools) in accomplishing one of your three goals, in constructing the new you. After you have completed your lists study them carefully. If you think an additional tool would help accomplish a goal, add it to your list.

Variations:

Complete Activity One with a partner who can help you, especially in the task of developing that comprehensive list of tools at your disposal. In this activity, you are still focusing upon your personal goals, tools, and actions.

Complete Activity One with a friend who lacks self-confidence, who does not set out to accomplish significant goals. Helping your friend with these lists can be a helpful step in self-development for both of you.

2. ACTIVITY TWO:

First, think of which room in your house held the happiest memories for you when you were about twelve. Draw the room, placing the furniture as best you can recall. List the people that were in the room most frequently. List the activities that most frequently occurred there. List the reasons the room was such a special place for you. Now, think about your world today. Draw a room in your current house that you want to make into your most special room. What furniture will you place there? What people will your place there? What activities will you undertake there?

This exercise reminds us that the practice of reminiscence is often promoted among older adults as a therapeutic intervention, as a mechanism for affirming the values within a person's biography, and as a means of insuring continuity.

WORKSHEET 3.5

Three activities are offered for exploring the fifth principle, that "Life experience is the foundation and resource for all learning."

1. ACTIVITY ONE:

Five individuals have just arrived for an orientation program for new employees at the corporate reservations center of a national hotel/motel chain. Each new employee has a unique history because of past life experiences and will enter the orientation program with a different set of resources for learning new positions as reservations clerks. They may also enter the orientation program with some "baggage," past learned behaviors or attitudes, that may have to be unlearned if the new employee is to become proficient in accomplishing the responsibilities of the new position.

Below are a position description for corporate reservations clerks and brief profiles of the five new employees. Your task as a member of a problem-solving group is to determine what elements (skills, attitudes, knowledge) from each individual's background are relevant to the new position and should be considered by the training staff. Since the profiles are brief, you must make certain reasonable assumptions about excluded information.

Position Description for Reservations Clerks:

Minimum requirements: (1) at least the equivalent of a high school diploma; (2) no major speech, hearing, vision, or motor defects that cannot be accommodated by assistive devices available at corporate headquarters; (3) and able to speak, read, and write in the English language.

Position Responsibilities:

(1) answer incoming telephone calls from customers for reservations nationwide; (2) use the reservations computer system to enter, change, or cancel reservations; (3) use the reservations computer system to make special reservation notations; (3) use the reservations computer system to assign appropriate

rates; (4) use the reservations computer system to identify locator maps and travel directions from various points; (4) handle the most commonly occurring inquiries, requests, and complaints; and (5) refer to an appropriate supervisor those special and occasional inquiries, requests, and complaints that cannot be routinely handled.

Applicant 1:

Jolene, female, 65 years of age, received her GED six years ago, widowed for three years, never worked outside the home, for many years volunteered as a cook's assistant for the local school lunch program, volunteered as a teacher's aide in first grade for four years, raised four children, uses a hearing aid.

Applicant 2:

Marcus, male, 72 years of age, completed high school at age 16, has worked as a customer representative in a regional employment office for his entire career, has worked for five years as a part-time reservations clerk at a local motel after his retirement; has volunteered during the past five years as a senior mentor for at-risk students in the public school. Has raised two children, needs no assistive devices. His wife needs assistance in daily living activities.

Applicant 3:

Tillie, female, 58 years of age; completed high school in Mexico City; is bilingual; moved to Texas at age 22; taught Spanish as a volunteer in the middle school in her community, provided staff development programs for middle school faculty in the Hispanic culture; husband is living and is still working in the oil industry; has traveled extensively with her husband; no children; is in excellent health; loves working with people, and presents herself as a very warm and caring person.

Applicant 4:

Will, male, 72 years of age; has never completed high school; worked as a night supply clerk in a wholesale outlet establishment until the work got to be too much for him physically; wife taught him to read and to work numbers; has never pursued completion of his

GED although the director of the local literacy coalition interviewed Will and informed him that he would probably pass the GED if he would come for the five GED review sessions provided locally; Will was afraid he would not pass, so did not pursue the opportunity. Will needs to supplement his income and believes that this new job is just the ticket for him, Will has good organizational skills, he likes to work alone.

Applicant 5:

Lolla, female, 84 years of age; worked for about 8 years as a young girl in housekeeping at a girls' sorority in the neighboring university town; worked the remainder of her career in custodial work at the university; retired 14 years ago at 70, in fairly good health; obtained GED through the university human resources department before retirement; divorced as a middle-aged woman and has supported herself ever since. Lolla is responsible and likes challenges. When she retired from the university, she had no complaints in her personnel file and many strong letters of commendation.

Create a separate page for each applicant. Use the following format to identify the assets and/or liabilities of each applicant.

Assets: knowledge, skills, values, personal qualities developed through life experience which might assist in preparing for the new career:

1. ______________________________
2. ______________________________
3. ______________________________
4. ______________________________
5. ______________________________

Liabilities: knowledge, skills, values, personal qualities developed through life experience which might interfere in preparing for the new career:

1. ______________________________
2. ______________________________
3. ______________________________

4. ______________________________________

5. ______________________________________

Compare the lists. Discuss specifically the role of experience in contributing to learning throughout life.

2. ACTIVITY TWO:

Point to a specific occasion when an event in your life involved a difficult circumstance or a loss. Describe something you learned from that experience that has helped you since. How did it help you? Can what you have learned be used to help another person?

3. ACTIVITY THREE:

Identify a new role which you have assumed or will assume. What in your personal experience may assist or inhibit you in learning your new role? Would sharing your experience with another person help you understand it better?

WORKSHEET 3.6

Principle six states that "Personal and social contexts affect learning."

The state extension service is starting a new program designed to help county residents work together to build safer communities. You are a member of the team which has agreed to poll the elders of the county regarding their perceptions of safety problems and concerns.

Complete the following activity first from the perspective of a rural farming county, then from the perspective of a major metropolitan county.

Step One: Brainstorm a list of factors which contribute to shaping one's personal and social context or world, such as economic status, social relationships, physical well-being, housing, transportation, access to services, cultural and recreational activities, religious affiliation, work opportunities, family and friendship relationships, and other factors you might wish to list.

Step Two: List those problems or concerns that might be mentioned by the seniors.

For each problem or concern listed, indicate what the appropriate response might be: education, action, or some combination of education and action.

CHAPTER 4

Twelve Principles Integrated

In the previous two chapters, twelve principles were presented, six from the perspective of adult development and six from the perspective of adult learning. Our task in this chapter is fourfold. First, we highlight the relationships between and among these principles. Second, we offer a mandate for action which logically flows from these principles. Third, we provide examples of the continuum of connections with older adults encountered by helpers. Fourth, we identify existing patterns that help us connect with older adults.

RELATIONSHIPS AMONG PRINCIPLES

Figure 4.1 represents the interplay of adult learning and adult development principles in support of successful aging.

The first pair of principles, namely that "Aging is a developmental process" and that "Learning is a process involving multiple personal changes," provides a foundation for all of the remaining principles. Each learner has a need to know and a need to change specific to his or her developmental stage. To support the learner's developmental growth, the helper needs to clarify the types of change and learning that are required, ranging from a new behavior to a pervasive restructuring in attitudes, values, or sense of self. For example, the individual may desire a minor lifestyle change such as remembering to leave a light on or a major change such as adjusting to the loss of a partner. The helpful practitioner begins by identifying the unique demands for change presented to the individual as a re-

1. Aging is a developmental process.
   Learning is a process involving multiple personal changes.
2. Each older adult is unique.
   Individual needs, emotions, and approaches to learning shape the learning experience.
3. Older adults should maximize physiological and psychological capacities.
   Learning capacity is adequate for meeting life challenges.
4. Locus of control is a central issue throughout life.
   The learner actively constructs the future.
5. Continuity of self is lifelong.
   Life experience is the foundation and resource for all learning.
6. Older adults need to be meaningfully connected.
   Personal and social contexts affect learning.

Figure 4.1 The integration of adult learning principles and adult development principles.

sult of transitions during older adulthood. These foundational principles apply equally well to us as developing individuals. Would that they were applied to all of our challenges for change.

The second pair of principles, that "each older adult is unique" and that "individual needs, emotions and approaches to learning shape the learning experience," informs a helping individual that the task is to explore the personal world of each older adult. An older adult may seem polite and formal—often a cohort phenomenon—but he or she may indeed wish to talk about a loss or a fear. Time and patience will contribute to a helping relationship. It behooves the practitioner to give the older adult the fullest opportunity to share and to develop trust. For all individuals to grow and flourish, they must be respected as unique individuals. As caring helpers, we should become progressively skilled in identifying assets unique to all those with whom we interact. Only after taking time to study an older person's world, should we being making suggestions about learning activities such as nutritional intervention or safety adaptations in existing housing.

The third pair of principles, that "older adults should maximize physiological and psychological capacities" and that "learning capacity is adequate for meeting life challenges" are essential to bear in mind. Older adults must not be made to feel they are incapable of learning, despite what the myths of aging suggest. The best advice that we could offer is advice that is appropriate for persons of all ages; namely, use whatever capacities exist at any given time in response to whatever context or challenge presents itself. It is through use that capacities become strengthened, and it is through application to many different challenges that capacities become flexible and adaptable. Developing strategies for reducing or eliminating fat from one's favorite recipes sets the stage for a more pervasive sensitivity, such as looking for the hidden and somewhat concealed presence of fat in processed foods purchased in the supermarket.

The fourth pair of principles, that "locus of control is a central issue throughout life" and that "the learner actively constructs the future," are connected in perspective. Older adults have internal drives to take charge of how they will live and what personal decisions they will make. This is natural and normal as individuals progress from infancy into old age. Although there may be situations in which this capacity is somewhat diminished, the helping person continually seeks avenues for fostering a robust degree of individual autonomy. Choice in clothing, furnishings, and personal decorative items is important to the mental well-being of individuals who have had to make the decision to move to an assisted living facility. Control over one's daily schedule, activities, hobbies, and diet are important to persons of all ages, the elderly included.

The fifth pair of principles, that "continuity of self is lifelong" and that "life experience is the foundation and resource for all learning," confirms the individuality and personal growth potential for each learner over time, no matter what the chronological age. These principles focus attention on the importance of recognizing and respecting the totality of an individual's life. All individuals are the sum total of all of their pervious experiences. Further, from their past, individuals are able to derive strength and meaning as they continually redefine themselves in the present. This is particularly helpful as a coping mechanism where memory of "getting through a tough time" in the past can serve as a tonic to an older adult's lagging self-esteem due to a loss or medical condition. Many times, clothing from a particular period of one's life is favored and worn well after the styles have been discarded by the fashion industry. Many times also, music which surrounded one during one's youth resonates as no music from subsequent eras ever could. A caring person will search for opportunities to support those themes, experiences, and values which have had meaning through major stages of one's life.

The final pair of principles, that "older adults need to be meaningfully connected" and that "personal and social contexts affect learning," speak to the fact that all persons, not simply the elderly, are social beings. Persons are most fully human when they are most fully in touch with and immersed with others in their personal worlds. We develop and refine both our sense of self (self-concept) as well as our sense of worth (self-esteem) in relation to others and our world. For an older adult this may mean being called upon as advisor, tutor, babysitter, part-time or fill-in worker, volunteer, or participant in family or community decision making. As helping persons we surely recognize the importance of these two principles in our own personal lives; efforts should be made to ensure that these principles are applied to the elderly whose lives we touch.

MANDATE FOR ACTION

Collectively, these six sets of principles provide a strong mandate for action. They speak to us about the inherent needs and possibilities of all adults, older adults included, for growth, individuality, competence, autonomy, wholeness, and engagement. The framework for connecting with older adults provides for a wide range of educational responses and approaches. Within the six principles, nearly every issue and concern of learning and aging can be addressed.

Figure 4.2 juxtaposes the two sets of principles. It shows the relationship between the principles derived from the distinct yet interrelated disciplines of gerontology and adult education. They are bound by their singular focus upon the mature adult. Figure 4.2 highlights the six functions these principles serve in supporting and enhancing personal growth and development. These principles, a strong yet supple interconnected system, serve to shape our values and guide our practice; they provide the paths to enable us as caring helpers to connect with and support the older adult.

These twelve principles fortify the helping professional, the caring individual, and the older adult alike with a firmly grounded set of core beliefs. These core beliefs—principles—when fully embraced, are logically accompanied with a congruent, constructive and positive array of emotions, which in turn, predispose the helping individual to make meaningful connections which support and enhance the lives of older adults. In sum, the mandate for action involves developing firmly established attitudes, including beliefs, emotions, and predispositions to act.

What we propose is deceptively simple! We are inviting all helping individuals to think, feel and act in three dimensions of time: proactively, actively, and retroactively in supporting the lives of older adults.

In the proactive sense, as helping individuals we need to think, feel, and act in ways that activate, anticipate, expect, and explore the future potential which all persons have—including ourselves as well as elders—for growth, individuality, competence, autonomy, wholeness, and engagement.

Perhaps the best way to appreciate this concept is to explore our own sense of growing older. Will we want to rise on someone else's time schedule, or on our own? Will we change? How will we want to be seen? Consider the following true story:

> Madelyn R., a well-meaning volunteer in a senior housing complex, met Mrs. Figeroa, a 76 year old widow of Portuguese heritage. Concerned about Mrs. Figeroa's state of mind and wishing to help her, Madelyn determined that she would convince Mrs. Figeroa to wear brighter colors. She was able to get a local department store to donate a charming pink pant suit and matching blouse. When presented with this unexpected gift of concern and consideration, Mrs. Figeroa went up to her apart-

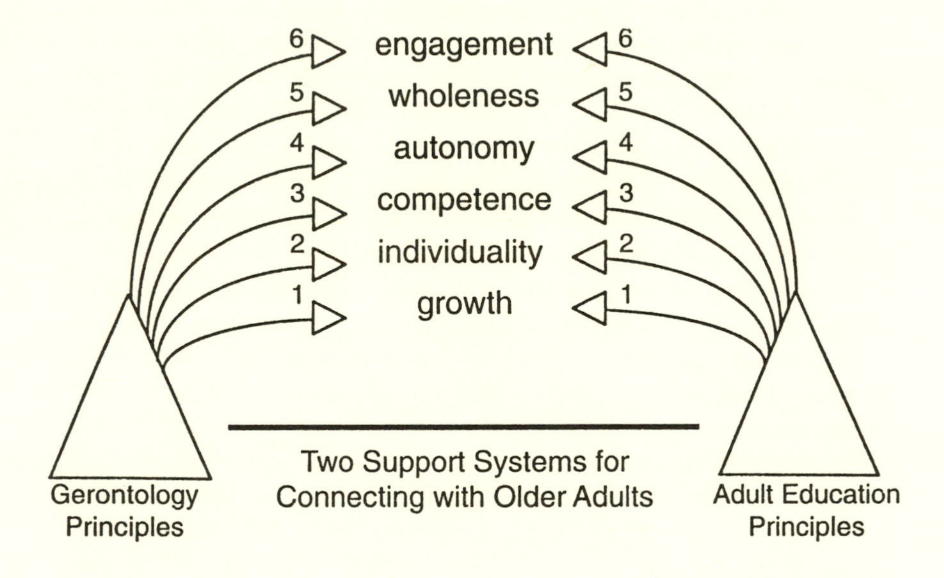

Figure 4.2 The relationship between the sets of principles and the lives of older adults.

> ment and changed into the new outfit. When she returned to the social area in the lobby, everyone clapped. Madelyn R. was delighted and felt quite proud of her intervention.
>
> As soon as Madelyn R. left, however, Mrs. Figeroa returned to her apartment, changed back into her black dress and declared, "Just let me know when Madelyn's coming back and I'll put the pink outfit back on again."

In the active sense, as helping individuals we need to think, feel, and act in ways that enhance, facilitate, foster, and support the constructive life-style choices and developments of the elderly for growth, individuality, competence, autonomy, wholeness, and engagement.

> We might wonder for example, why Madelyn R., a well-educated individual did not inquire of Mrs. Figeroa, "Would you like to change your style?" and "Could I be of some assistance in shopping for you?" Then Mrs. Figeroa might have said, "No, dear, in my country older widows wear black to show that they loved their husbands. I honor my husband, that is the tradition. Besides I don't like pants; they bind my legs."

In the retroactive sense, as helping individuals we need to think, feel, and act in ways that affirm, celebrate, respect, and reinforce efforts which already have been made by the elderly to achieve their fullest potential for growth, individuality, competence, autonomy, wholeness, and engagement.

> Madelyn R. might have said, "Really? Mrs. Figeroa, how many children do you have, how many grandchildren, and sisters? Is your whole family in this country? Please tell me about your life." And Mrs. Figeroa would have had a nicer day. She would have prepared her special coffee, shared her expertise in widowing, and made a friend.

Connecting does not mean taking over for another. We make a mistake in assuming that others should do what we would wish to do if we ourselves were elders. Connecting is a co-contributing way of responding and approaching in which the helper receives and learns as well.

Connecting with older adults is made possible when caring

individuals understand and interrelate in the real world the principles which come from the literature of theory and research in adult development and adult learning. These principles provide a framework from within which helpers can touch the lives of many older adults.

For each principle there exists a number of actions (proactive, active, and retroactive) which will support the active growth and development of persons.

Connecting with Older Adults

Those in a position to help older adults must recognize that the desire or need to learn springs from at least three sources:

1. *The individual need to know.* This category includes personal objectives such as learning how to drive or how to cook tamales with fat-free ingredients.

- *The community need to know.* This category includes a broad range of community responses to the aging population such as making adjustments in a housing complex in order to retain the older residents, or dealing with crime and safety issues.
- *The cohort need to know.* This category includes role changes which range from being informed medical consumers to managing financial, household, and maintenance chores formerly handled by a spouse. While gender roles were often traditional for the current cohort of older adults, women, now widowed, may need to develop skills that were once deemed "masculine."

Patterns of Helping

Certain patterns will emerge as helpers apply the adult development and adult learning principles. These are the major steps in the pattern of helping older adults:

- Acknowledge the developmental challenge or opportunity.
- Identify the demands for change that the challenge or opportunity presents.
- Encourage and assist the individual to bridge the change through his or her own strengths.
- Ascertain the need to connect with other helping sources (including professional and nonprofessional support systems).
- Begin the networking process to facilitate the connection.

How a pattern of learning activity develops will depend not only upon the individual, cohort, or community need to know but also upon the functional status of the older adult; namely, independent, needing some assistance, or highly dependent.

The following section, Part III, helps adult education practitioners and other concerned individuals develop the capacity to enhance the lives of older adults.

Part III

Entering the World of Practice

Part III, Entering the World of Practice, develops in Chapter 5 guidelines applicable to a range of settings and situations for helpers who need to make connections with older adults. Examples are provided to illustrate the forging of positive connections. In Chapter 6, we enter the private lives of real people, the cohort of today's older adults. This chapter allows the reader to connect in various ways with real situations that we have encountered in our practice.

CHAPTER 5

Making Connections Happen

Our lives present us with countless opportunities for connecting with older adults. The challenge in this regard is twofold: first, to recognize the opportunities around us; and second, to select approaches and strategies which support older adults in the process of successful aging. After addressing these challenges, we will give illustrations of how caregivers can effect positive connections.

RECOGNIZING OPPORTUNITIES

How do we identify opportunities? Of many possibilities, two approaches are especially fruitful avenues to explore. These involve focusing upon the social roles we play and upon the life transitions of the older adults with whom we interact in these roles.

Social Roles

Each of the multiple roles we play in life establishes expectations, presents occasions for social interaction, and links us to one or more "role partners." At any given moment, we may be spouse, mother, grandmother, sister, daughter, cousin, distant relative, merchant, service provider or consumer, doctor, volunteer, neighbor, supervisor, assistant, confidante, pastor, teacher, casual acquaintance, caregiver, or friend. In those roles we face the challenge of responding appropriately to those with whom we interact.

Life Transitions

Our society has been described as one in which we are in transition throughout our lives. We are usually able to point to a life circumstance or event which serves as a trigger for the process of transition. The "trigger event" may be a change which we have deliberately caused or an unintended event which requires us to adjust to a new situation. Trigger events and transitions in the lives of the older adults constitute "teachable moments." At these times helping persons can provide valuable assistance.

SELECTING APPROACHES AND STRATEGIES

How do we select productive approaches and strategies for the continued learning and development of those seniors whom we encounter daily? We must answer several questions: Which principles are most relevant to the opportunity presented to us? Who are the older adults? How will we connect and interact with them? What pattern of assistance is most appropriate?

Relevant Principles

Twelve principles for practice have been presented: six principles of aging and six principles of adult learning. The relationships among these principles have been explored, and six general principles for practice have been developed. Review the principles to determine which ones are most relevant to the challenge or opportunity you are facing. Once you have selected the most appropriate principle or principles to maximize, you have a framework for making further decisions. The principles again, are:

1. Aging is a developmental process.

   Learning is a process involving multiple personal changes.

2. Each older adult is unique.

   Individual needs, emotions, and approaches to learning shape the learning experience.

3. Older adults should maximize physiological and psychological capacities.

   Learning capacity is adequate for meeting life challenges.

4. Locus of control is a central issue throughout life.

   The learner actively constructs the future.

5. Continuity of self is lifelong.

   Life experience is the foundation and resource for all learning.

6. Older adults need to be meaningfully connected.

   Personal and social contexts affect learning.

Older Adults

Of the many ways to describe the older adults with whom we enter into helping relationships, three are most useful in helping us to understand the elderly not only as a special segment of contemporary society but also as unique individuals.

The simplest is to identify the present functional status of the elderly individual: independent, in need of assistance, or dependent. An independent older adult is physically and psychologically capable of taking care of himself or herself in accomplishing activities of daily living (ADL's). At the other end of the continuum, a dependent older adult is, because of either physical or psychological limitations, incapable of taking care of the most fundamental of the activities of daily living. Between these two functional states is the older adult in need of some assistance.

Second, we can use age as a clue to other issues for an individual at a particular stage in life. With increasing age, one can reasonably expect a change in focus and perspective on a number of issues such as grandparenting, retirement and productive employment, personal health and well-being, housing, significant relationships, and social networks.

Last, older adults can be described according to a diverse set of factors including economic status, living arrangements, cultural values, marital status, race and ethnicity, educational background, religious and political affiliations, rural or urban residential community, individual patterns of adaptation and aging, and housing arrangements.

In reflecting on one of these three approaches, consider the applicable principle or principles for practice.

Individual Need-to-Know Approach

Interact with the older adult—often a family member or friend by using an individualized approach. One focuses upon a specific individual to achieve a positive personal change. This approach may be subtle or direct, involving clearly defined contacts and agreements about the agenda for change.

Cohort Need-to-Know Approach

Group members of an age cohort and provide them with collective support services and programs as they face common challenges of productive change. This approach is typically undertaken by an organization or by a formal or informal group within the community.

Community Need-to-Know Approach

Integrate age groups if members of a given community need to interact over a common challenge to produce change.

This approach involves the greatest diversity of participants and presents the greatest risk of failure to connect with the individual as a focus of change.

Assistance Pattern

The pattern of helping is appropriate whether we are assisting an older adult to capitalize upon a positive opportunity for growth and development or working with an individual to overcome a deficiency, face a dilemma, or address a deep-seated need. The pattern can be entered and exited at any point depending on the situation:

a. identify barriers to a helping role,

b. reduce or eliminate barriers as possible,

c. establish a relationship of trust and credibility,

d. acknowledge unique developmental challenges or opportunities,

e. identify the type of demand for change that the unique developmental challenge or opportunity presents,

f. encourage and assist the individual to bridge the change through his or her own strength,

g. provide information regarding alternatives and resources as needed,

h. guide the individual in the pursuit of alternative avenues of change,

i. ascertain the need to connect with other sources of assistance and support,

j. begin the networking process to facilitate the connection,

k. provide direct service or assistance in embarking upon the change process,

l. encourage the individual as change is undertaken, and

m. follow up as the individual works through the process of consolidating change into the life-style.

MAKING CONNECTIONS HAPPEN

In order to connect with older adults, each of us must recognize opportunities and select approaches and strategies. Our efforts may be facilitated by the following examples of how others have been able to develop connections with older adults.

School Superintendent: Narrative Case Study

Marlene Thompson has been the superintendent of a large urban school district for six years. She has brought excellence to the district and instilled pride in the staff. In addition, she has worked hard to establish a positive environment for all staff members. The teachers often refer to Marlene as a friend and mentor as well as a boss. Her personnel director recently informed her that fifteen teachers plan to retire during the next two school years. Concerned about the loss of teachers and about the district's ability to help them make this transition, she has organized an informal luncheon for these senior faculty members with the following agenda: to discuss what the teachers hoped to achieve through retirement, to identify the kind of support services they would appreciate at this point, to determine the future retirees' level of interest for continued involvement with the school district, to brainstorm a range of alternative positions and staffing patterns to allow for their continued employment in some capacity, and to establish a task force to determine preretirement career paths and postretirement career alternatives.

Discussion of these issues revealed that none of the teachers felt adequately prepared to face the transition; only two seemed to comprehend the financial implications of their retirement decision. Most had not thought out what they would be doing from day to day to make their lives meaningful. Several had worried at length about being around their retired husbands twenty-four hours a day! Of the fifteen teachers, only five were uninterested in maintaining any formal employment relationship with the district; even those five expressed sincere desire to volunteer when it didn't conflict with travel plans, health demands, or additional family obligations. The other teachers spoke of their interest in maintaining a different type of working relationship with the school district. Several had already spoken among themselves about the desirability of job sharing. The possibility of splitting the academic year, splitting the work day, or splitting the work week all generated enthusiasm. Several teachers looked favorably upon being paired with new teachers as mentors; others found appealing the possibility of joining central district staff in curriculum design or staff development areas on a part-time basis. All supported the notion of career development workshops for the mature employee, including teaching and nonteaching personnel. They also felt that a life planning workshop ought to be available to all employees at selected times in their careers. Two teachers indicated willingness to work part-time during the summer to move these ideas forward.

Expressing surprise that this type of meeting had not taken place long before, the superintendent committed herself to take the necessary administrative action to facilitate these possibilities. She affirmed that the meeting would set the stage for real policy initiatives, that the school district would act to turn the creative ideas into reality, and that more meetings would be scheduled to support personnel in their career and personal decisions.

After the meeting, Marlene took several actions. She contacted the state department of education to see whether they would fund an unsolicited proposal related to career paths for mature faculty; briefed the president of the school board on her plans to employ two teachers part-time in the summer to work on an administrative research and development project; and indicated that at the end of this period a full report and proposal would be placed before the board.

We leave the story as it unfolds.

School Superintendent: Analysis

Marlene's concern about losing valued teachers to retirement motivated her to call a meeting. Although she could not predict the outcome, she knew she wanted to be involved as her teachers focused on their future. This meeting was her opportunity to connect with older adults. She saw in their transition from employment to retirement an important challenge and teachable moment.

Marlene selected appropriate approaches and strategies for making connections with older adults. Principles two, four, and five appear especially relevant in this situation. Marlene did not presume to know exactly how each of her senior teachers would respond to the prospect of retirement. Instead, she gave them autonomy in shaping the change process. She knew that her teachers understood their needs regarding the pending transition, the emotions which would play into the transition, and the individual approaches that would be most supportive for their successful transition. Any unilateral initiative on the part of the superintendent would have been unlikely to fit individuals in their unique circumstances.

Marlene also recognized several truths: 1) the value to the district of the teachers' professional experience, 2) their capability for full and independent functioning, 3) the need for continued cognitive functioning after retirement, 4) and the importance of providing for continuity in the face of a pending transition. She chose to meet with the teachers as a cohort and felt that they had a shared learning agenda. The connection approach was reasonable and readily accessible to the superintendent.

Last, having established herself as an administrator to be trusted, Marlene faced no barriers in this regard. She moved unobtrusively through most of the remaining steps by providing assistance without negating the centrality of the teachers' roles in shaping their change process. In essence, Marlene became a partner, not the primary architect, that role being appropriate for the senior teachers.

Community Recreation Department Codirectors: Narrative Case Study

Ben and Lisa Stuart recently graduated from college with undergraduate degrees in recreation and community development. Subsequently, they were hired as a team to direct the recreation department of a southwestern city and were given a mandate to build an exemplary recreation program. The city administration was committed to maximize the use of its recreation facilities for all members of the community. The recreation facilities and programs were to become the model for other midsized communities in the Sunbelt. The newly elected mayor, having a professional background in physical education, promised in his campaign to bring good things back to the community—for people and with people. He also promised fiscal restraint in all his undertakings.

The history of the recreation department reflected current dissatisfaction. The community had voted down several bond issues to develop a plan for the facilities constructed during boom times; thus the department had assumed a custodial role regarding the facilities under its management. Citizens believed that they never got their money's worth from the expenditures and feared a large tax increase would accompany an improvement plan.

During the first weeks on the job, Ben and Lisa took stock of the recreation facilities, conducted site visits and informal interviews with users, and reviewed past usage records.

They learned that a number of the facilities had fallen into disrepair. The community had two fine swimming pools, both in excellent condition; an 18-hole golf course with excellent access and parking; a deed to 42 acres of undeveloped forest-grassland with a small lake, which could be developed for recreational fishing, swimming, and boating; three bike and two walking trails, all overgrown; one large amphitheater; two public picnic areas with covered eating facilities and restrooms; one modest community access recreation center with four separate meeting rooms and a large hall; outdoor playing areas for baseball, volleyball, basketball, football, and hockey. All of these facilities needed a facelift. At least half of the facilities had become hangouts for youth gangs and were no longer frequented by other segments of the community who felt neither welcome nor safe there. Most adults felt that there was no reason for them to go to the facilities, and the other adults believed that the facilities were designed for the younger set. No programming initiatives had been undertaken by the department over the past six or seven years. In short, while the recreation department had great problems, it also had great potential. According to the mayor, only through voluntary community support could its potential to be realized.

Ben and Lisa established a representative advisory board for the department. The board identified three goals as central to all of the department's undertakings:

1. To provide opportunities at each facility and within each program for all persons within the community—for youths, young adults, and mature adults; for all persons regardless of skill levels; and for all persons regardless of their functional levels.

2. To upgrade all facilities to good repair (barrier-free status).

3. To work with businesses and individuals within the community, and to provide a wide range of volunteer opportunities.

During the year the board functioned as two teams in implementing these three goals. The mission team assumed responsibility for developing and overseeing programs and recruiting and training instructional staff. The management team assumed responsibility for developing and overseeing facilities and addressing additional administrative issues. After each team prepared its one-year report addressing the goals, Ben and Lisa combined them into a single report, indicating the large contributions made by older adults:

Goal 1: Community-Wide Access to Facilities and Programs

- Forty-five percent of the older adults within the community participated in age-integrated activities

including walking, safe cook-out, beginning swimmers, nature watercolor, a "songs of Great Outdoors" community sing program, a wheelchair walk, life saving, boat safety, and animal grooming.
- Twenty-one percent of the older adults within the community participated in age-segregated activities including vegetable gardening, mature adult water exercise, teaching conservation to the grandchildren, and writing stories of the way things were.
- Twenty-seven percent of the volunteer leaders for all programs were older adults themselves.

Goal 2: Facilities Upgrading
- All facilities have been given a facelift and made barrier-free.
- Sixty-two percent of individuals volunteering time to assist in upgrading and maintaining facilities were older adults.

Goal 3: Community Support
- All community groups supporting older adults responded affirmatively to requests to make special contributions—money, in-kind services, and volunteer hours—to the department.

Ben and Lisa's report was well received, and administration expressed optimism about the future of the model program.

Community Recreation Department Codirectors: Analysis

Ben and Lisa took seriously their mandate to place the department at the service of the entire community. They worked hard with other like-minded persons who saw inclusiveness as one of the hallmarks of excellence. To help them reach their goal, they identified opportunities for connecting with older adults. Although there is no evidence that older adults' life transitions provided the stimulus for program initiatives, Ben and Lisa clearly recognized as an asset the fact that senior citizens typically have more leisure time. They regarded older adults as likely participants in programs that were perceived as meeting their needs, and as willing contributors to undertakings that they viewed as valuable.

Ben and Lisa selected appropriate approaches and strategies to revitalize their recreation department, its facilities, and its programs. Principles one, three, four and six appear especially relevant. Department programs were designed to meet developmental issues and interests, but the department did not assume that all programs and associated learning needed to reflect the developmental perspective. Consequently, both age-segregated and age-integrated programs were offered. The physiological and psychological capacities of older adults can continue to function well into older adulthood and can be tapped and maximized through their use.

Further, the entire recreational program is constructed to help not only older adults, but all members of the community, to make a meaningful connection with others. Older adults are grouped in these programs as cohorts in the age-segregated programming activities, as community groups in the age-integrated programming activities, and both as community groups and individuals in much of the faculty and staff orientation and instructor training. Ben and Lisa's patterns of assistance are not clearly delineated in the telling of the story; in actuality, they became full partners with all members of the community, a role that enhanced the quality of the outcome.

OTHER ISSUES TO BE EXPLORED

To this point, we have discussed two specific connections, one emerging from issues associated with employment and the other emerging from issues associated with recreation. Many additional issues could be addressed concerning both employment and recreation. Other connections can also be made around issues related to family, religion or spirituality, health, the media, education, social networks, and community participation. The next section, Chapter 6, will introduce some older adults. Let us consider when and if and how we might develop strategies to connect with these individuals. Let us explore educational responses and approaches. Again, our challenge is twofold: first, to recognize the opportunities around us; and second, to select approaches and strategies which support older adults in the process of successful aging.

CHAPTER 6

Vignettes with Reflections

This chapter presents ten slice-of-life stories about older persons' lives. These vignettes may be used by individuals, groups, or classes to develop strategies for educational responses and approaches. Take time with each one: we recommend one vignette per class session. There are no "right answers," only suggestions as to how helping persons can connect with the older persons and provide support for change. Furthermore, your answers will differ according to your relationship to the individuals in the vignettes. In some cases you may conclude that no change is required. Consult the strategies in Chapter 5 and the 12 principles of aging and learning (see Figure 4.1) as guidelines in exploring connections with these older persons.

MARIA AND TOMAS BENITO

Maria and Tomas, both in their eighties, have just celebrated their 64th wedding anniversary. They are in good health and live independently in their small 50-year-old wood frame home. Their community of two thousand people, mostly older adults, is located in a rural farming county in the Southwest. Tomas receives social security, and they have a small reserve in savings to meet emerging needs. Tomas does not receive a pension, nor does he have a substantial retirement nest egg. Deeply religious, Maria regards the church as a very important part of her life. Tomas is interested in spiritual development and is valued as a "good and just man" among members of the community. Formal church participation, however, is less important to him.

Their four children have long since moved away to major metropolitan areas. Now living at least a six-hour drive from the homestead, they have all acquired trades and are members of lower middle-income families. Over the years, the Benitos seem to have become strangers to their four children. Maria and Tomas rarely see them and have only occasional notes and Christmas greetings from their ten grandchildren and their sixteen great grandchildren. Both Maria and Tomas write; however, the children don't answer their letters. The older Benitos do not drive any longer and can not afford to make frequent long distance telephone calls.

Maria and Tomas are lonely. They yearn for the old times when family was the most important thing in their lives, when as many as twenty people would gather together in the small home for important family celebrations. This was also the tradition in their parents' homes. Marriages, birthdays, first communions, and graduations meant a lot of hard work but happy times with all the family "gathered in." Maria and Tomas anguish about what they feel they must have done or failed to do, causing their family to drift apart. They worry that the values and traditions in their family and their culture will vanish. They worry about what will happen to them if they need additional help in meeting the demands of daily living. They worry too about the younger generations, and what values will serve as their anchors in times of need.

Reflection

Describe what is going on here.
Identify who you are and your relationship to the older adults in the story.
Describe how this vignette presents an opportunity to make a connection. Consider these older adults' roles and the life transitions they are experiencing.
What conversation would you have with them?
Describe the approaches and strategies you would use to connect with these older adults. Remember the principles, the functional status, the need-to-know, and patterns of assistance.
Identify other individuals who could make an appropriate connection to these older adults.

CLAIRE JOHNSON

At 72, Claire is an attractive, healthy, comfortably situated widow living in a retirement home outside a major southwestern city. Her husband died a year ago when he suffered a massive coronary shortly after they had embarked in their recreational vehicle to visit their two children over a thousand miles away.

In the intervening months Claire has grieved the loss of her husband and, with the help of her children, has begun to consider how she will spend the rest of her life. As a young mother, Claire was renowned as a story teller. She was able not only to read children's stories with enchantment and wonder, but also to weave a tale for any occasion. She had stories of hurt fingers healing magically, of lost kittens being found, of birthday candles as big as trees, and of vacations to far-off places.

Claire has decided to embark on a career to produce stories for young people. With her children helping jog her memory, she will recreate her tales of long ago. Because of their professional skills, her children will also be will be happy to assist in the illustrations for the publication and the marketing. Claire will enroll in a creative writing workshop at a branch of the local community college and will hire a young neighbor to help her get started in word processing and desk top publishing.

People in local community agencies, hearing of Claire's new venture, have asked her to contribute to their undertakings. She has been contacted by the adult day care center, the area agency on aging, the local newspaper, the local television station, the school district, the residential retirement community, the adult literacy council, the county rehabilitation clinics, and the Volunteer Action Center. For Claire this is the time for "giving back."

Reflection

Using the principles of aging and learning, describe what interventions, if any, you would consider using in this situation.

Describe what is going on here.
Identify who you are and your relationship to the older adult in the story.
Describe how this vignette presents an opportunity to make a connection. Consider this older adult's roles and the life transitions she is experiencing.
What conversation would you have with her?
Describe the approaches and strategies you would use to connect with these older adults. Remember the principles, the functional status, the need-to-know, and patterns of assistance.
Identify other individuals who could make an appropriate connection to this older adult.

ROBERT WILLIAMS

Robert is 92 years old. He graduated from high school and married his high school sweetheart over fifty years ago. Their little boy was the light of his life. Robert worked as a mechanic at a small auto repair shop during the early years of their marriage, but the marriage broke up after about five years when Robert was laid off; he has lost all contact with his former wife and his child.

Robert never remarried, always led a clean life, and considers himself a religious man although, as he explains, he hasn't been inside a church in many a year. He has worked as a mechanic for his entire work life. He still has friends among coworkers and customers but many of them are "dying off," as he puts it. Although he hasn't had steady work in twenty years, Robert still is known in the community as one of the best mechanics in the trade.

He lives in a high rise apartment complex less than a block away from the local coffee shop and the auto shop where he worked as a mechanic. Almost every day, Robert is able to walk with the help of a cane to the coffee shop for all the morning gossip. But he is becoming increasingly frail. Friends have heard that he fell twice on his way to morning coffee in the last few weeks. He is becoming forgetful as well. Not long ago the pharmacist found Robert wandering on the wrong street and helped him get to his coffee shop. Robert seems to have lost weight in the last few months also. Betty, his favorite waitress, gives him a snack to take home each morning. Robert has been telling people that he's not the man he used to be. He has also expressed the wish to do something for the younger generation growing up in the neighborhood before his time is up. While his spirits seem good, his body seems to be giving out.

Reflection

Using the principles of aging and learning, describe what interventions, if any, you would consider using in this situation.

Name your relationship to Robert Williams. Explore your strategies. Are there other people to include in your outreach connections? How does locus of control feature in Mr. Williams' situation?

Describe what is going on here.
Identify who you are and your relationship to the older adult in the story.
Describe how this vignette presents an opportunity to make a connection. Consider this older adult's roles and the life transitions he is experiencing.
What conversation would you have with him?
Describe the approaches and strategies you would use to connect with this older adult. Remember the principles, the functional status, the need-to-know, and patterns of assistance.
Identify other individuals who could make an appropriate connection to this older adult.

EILEEN SMITH

Eileen Smith, a 60-year-old, financially independent widow, lost her husband of 40 years in an accident two years ago. Subsequent to her loss she has participated in a local widow-to-widow program, sought assistance from its financial adviser regarding investments, and begun a widow-to-widow column as a freelance columnist.

After the death of her husband, she become even closer to her children and grandchildren. She was shocked to learn that her daughter and son-in-law were going to divorce and that her son-in-law was expected to receive custody of the two young children. Further, he planned to move out of state and start over with a new employer and an old romantic interest. She realized that she would no longer be seeing her grandchildren and that she would not be involved in "normal" grandparenting activities. This family change deeply affects her because she had expected to play a major role in her grandchildren's upbringing, and she strongly values family and continuity across generations.

Reflection

Using the principles of aging and learning, describe what interventions, if any, you would consider using in this situation.

Describe what is going on here.

Identify who you are and your relationship to the older adult in the story.

Describe how this vignette presents an opportunity to make a connection. Consider this older adult's roles and the life transitions she is experiencing.

What conversation would you have with her?

Describe the approaches and strategies you would use to connect with this older adult. Remember the principles, the functional status, the need-to-know, and patterns of assistance.

Identify other individuals who could make an appropriate connection to this older adult.

ROCCO AND RITA CONSUELO

Rocco and Rita Consuelo, both 82, are longtime owners of a "Mom and Pop" grocery store. Over the decades, they have become both sages and mentors for many of their friends and customers, mostly older adults themselves. Typically, either Rocco or Rita can be found with one or more people in deep conversation over a cup of coffee at the small table in the back of the store. Recently they were recommended by their pastor to participate in a week-long peer counseling training program at the local college. This program would prepare them as peer counselors and would involve four hours' service per week serving in a community agency. Their daughter is pleased to mind the store during their training and to relieve them during their hours as volunteers. They are concerned about their ability to serve in this volunteer role. They claim only to have "a love of their neighbors" and "good old common sense."

Reflection

Describe what is going on here.

Identify who you are and your relationship to the older adults in the story.

Describe how this vignette presents an opportunity to make a connection. Consider these older adults' roles and the life transitions they are experiencing.

What conversation would you have with them?

Describe the approaches and strategies you would use to connect with these older adults. Remember the principles, the functional status, the need-to-know, and patterns of assistance.

Identify other individuals who could make an appropriate connection to these older adults.

ALFREDO AND SYLVIA GARCIA

Alfredo, 75, and Sylvia Garcia, age 72, have just celebrated their 50th wedding anniversary. They have always lived in the small home built shortly after their marriage. Their five grown married children reside in different cities at least 200 miles away. Alfredo and Sylvia live on Alfredo's social security and money contributed each month from three of the five grown children.

Recently, the children held a family meeting and decided it was time to take over routine maintenance and upkeep of the house. Worried about the possibility of having the parents move in with one of them, they are experiencing caregiver stress.

Reflection

Describe what is going on here.
Identify who you are and your relationship to the older adults in the story.
Describe how this vignette presents an opportunity to make a connection. Consider these older adults' roles and the life transitions they are experiencing.
What conversation would you have with them?
Describe the approaches and strategies you would use to connect with these older adults. Remember the principles, the functional status, the need-to-know, and patterns of assistance.
Identify other individuals who could make an appropriate connection to these older adults.

TOMMY GRIMES

Mr. Grimes, age 86, lives alone in a single occupancy hotel in a northeastern city; he receives a seaman's pension. He has not seen his family in many years and feels no need to make contact with them. He enjoys playing cards and watching football games on television. Lately, however, he has experienced acute visual loss and arthritic pain that prevents him from engaging in routine activities. Consequently, he can no longer read, walk to the nearby grocery for food, or cook for himself on his small hot plate. He does not wish to leave the neighborhood, but would like to find a better living situation or at least some assistance.

Reflection

Describe what is going on here.

Identify who you are and your relationship to the older adult in the story.

Describe how this vignette presents an opportunity to make a connection. Consider this older adult's roles and the life transitions he is experiencing.

What conversation would you have with him?

Describe the approaches and strategies you would use to connect with this older adult. Remember the principles, the functional status, the need-to-know, and patterns of assistance.

Identify other individuals who could make an appropriate connection to this older adult.

HELEN VAN BRULEE

Helen Van Brulee, age 84, lives with her 67-year-old daughter, who actually seems to be the one in need of care. At 60, Irene injured her back in a car accident. From a subsequent lawsuit she received a handsome settlement. So, between the settlement and disability compensation payments, financial concerns are minimal for Irene. She is no longer able to walk and gets around in her wheelchair. Helen manages the house, shops, and cooks for the two women. Recently, however, she has suffered from fatigue. A social worker has counseled Helen to seek a long-term care institution for Irene and has recommended the family for assistance.

Reflection

Using the principles of aging and learning, describe what interventions, if any, you would consider using in this situation.

Describe what is going on here.

Identify who you are and your relationship to the older adult in the story.

Describe how this vignette presents an opportunity to make a connection. Consider this older adult's roles and the life transitions she is experiencing.

What conversation would you have with her?

Describe the approaches and strategies you would use to connect with this older adult. Remember the principles, the functional status, the need-to-know, and patterns of assistance.

Identify other individuals who could make an appropriate connection to this older adult.

WILLIAM AND SADIE STONE

William and Sadie Smith have been living for over a year in a subsidized senior housing complex in a major metropolitan city. They have made no friends. Neighbors have recently complained about loud arguments heard from their apartment. Family members, including two sons and a daughter who live in the area and who used to visit several times a week, come less and less frequently. The activity director has noticed that Sadie rarely leaves the apartment and that almost daily William makes his way past her office to the corner liquor store and returns with what looks like a "fifth."

Reflection

Describe what is going on here.
Identify who you are and your relationship to the older adults in the story.
Describe how this vignette presents an opportunity to make a connection. Consider these older adults' roles and the life transitions they are experiencing.
What conversation would you have with them?
Describe the approaches and strategies you would use to connect with these older adults. Remember the principles, the functional status, the need-to-know, and patterns of assistance.
Identify other individuals who could make an appropriate connection to these older adults.

MARTA BRUNNER

Marta Brunner is a healthy 60-year-old of German descent. She is the owner and operator of what is left of her family's six-acre ranch. She and several of her long-term women friends from the rural Christian Church established a Senior Adult Leadership Team (SALT), a group dedicated to locating out the frail elderly in the county and brokering services to meet their needs. In its first six months, SALT has grown by leaps and bounds. It has become the absorbing interest for Marta and her friends, who now spend several days a week managing the enterprise. She has thought about incorporating but is uncertain about what is involved.

Reflection

Using the principles of aging and learning, describe what interventions, if any, you would consider using in this situation.

Describe what is going on here.
Identify who you are and your relationship to the older adult in the story.
Describe how this vignette presents an opportunity to make a connection. Consider this older adult's roles and the life transitions she is experiencing.
What conversation would you have with her?
Describe the approaches and strategies you would use to connect with this older adult. Remember the principles, the functional status, the need-to-know, and patterns of assistance.
Identify other individuals who could make an appropriate connection to this older adult.

DISCUSSION

We have explored some of the issues and concerns that older people, their families, friends, and caregivers encounter through stories, vignettes. Each one presented a different issue and set of circumstances that might arise. If we were to see all of the social, psychological, and physical issues involved in growing old in one vignette, we might think that connecting would be overwhelming, but, in working on the situations in the vignettes, we found that each individual circumstance was approachable and often required little outreach. The strengths of the older persons themselves were ample. Using the principles of aging and learning as a metatheory allows us to develop educational approaches which enhance these innate strengths. If, for example, we stress the fourth pair of principles, "Locus of control is a central issue throughout life" and "The learner actively constructs the future," our responses would always be to place the decision-making, as much as possible, in the older adult's own hands.

Furthermore, we must ask, How *can* we make use of the background that we have developed to actually meet the needs of others? Who am *I* in the life of this person? What is a "helping person"? How can I truly connect?

If you are a professional, para-professional, volunteer, adult educator, family member with an interest in older persons, you may need to consider how to help, when to intervene, and when to react to situations involving older adults. This will depend on your relationship and the nature of your role in the older person's life.

Roles and Categories of Responses and Approaches

Our roles may differ from pastoral care worker, health care worker, human service provider, community/volunteer worker, family member, dietician, adult ed. teacher, older adult. Others, too, may need to learn about aging, including legal professionals, and airline personnel. Most individuals, because of their multiple roles in society, have almost limitless opportunities to support the process of successful aging for many older adults. Each one of us can be actively involved in creating life span development opportunities. Although you may have read several of the vignettes in this chapter and responded as neighbor, daughter, or in some professional capacity, you may now want to explore how your answers would differ if you imagined yourself in a different capacity.

In discussing the connections that helping persons can develop and maintain with older adults, we will need to differentiate the demands that mandate learning for development and adaptation. Our roles will depend on which category of learning need is indicated. The categories of educational responses and approaches previously explored are:

1.) *The individual need to know*, including personal learning objectives such as learning to drive or how to cook tamales using fat-free ingredients.

2.) *The community need to know*, encompassing a broad range of community responses to the aging population, from adjustments in a housing complex to crime and safety issues.

3.) *The cohort need to know*, involving role changes which range from informed medical consumerism to managing financial, household, and maintenance chores which had formerly been handled by a spouse.

Mutuality and Connections

Our responses to the vignettes—and to others we encounter—will depend on what level of involvement or connection we have or can have with each individual. We must recall that the second set of principles, "Each older adult is unique" and "Individual needs, emotions, and approaches to learning shape the learning experience," is also a valid process for ourselves as caring helpers. When we connect with older adults, we, too, will be engaged. We will make a friend, touch another's world, make our own lives better through the magic of mutuality and reciprocity. In putting the principles of aging and learning into practice, we will also learn about the world of aging—including our own.

Trust and Denial

In examining gerontological principles that can inform our practice as adult educators, we should also be aware of the powerful elements of trust and denial.

We don't often talk about trust. Yet the need for trust is at the center of all that we do. In our earliest moments and our last moments of life, we are dependent on trust. Every moment of risk, or relationship, or growth, is connected with trust. In *The Life Cycle Completed* Erik Erikson describes the basic "integrality" of life: each of us is dependent on *esperanza* (the Spanish word for hope). In growing older, we are reminded of the essential nature of trust: We are *all* aging, from the moment of birth. An essential part of life together is our commitment to care for one another.

Adult educators must remember the first pair of principles, "Aging is a developmental process," and "Learning is a process involving multiple personal changes." Each stage of life and each change that we have achieved play a significant part in our ability to grow. Trust, a feature of our first developmental stage, is i at each level of maturity.

As we trust our ability to learn about what others' actual needs may be, we will reflect on the second pair of principles, "Each older adult is unique," and "Individual needs, emotions, and approaches to learning shape the learning experience." We must learn to appreciate that the individuals we work with are truly that: individuals with unique approaches to life's changes. How have these elements come into play in your work with the vignettes?

Another issue to understand is the general cultural denial of aging: usually this comes from a wish that *we* stay the same, that those around us remain in place. Robert Butler noting this phenomenon in 1968, coined the word "ageism," which, he wrote, "reflects a deep seated uneasiness on the part of the young and middle-aged—a personal repulsion to and distaste for growing old, disease, disability; and fear of loss of powers, 'uselessness,' and death" (1982, p. 185). In reflecting on the third set of principles, "Older adults should maximize physiological and psychological capacities" and "Learning capacity is adequate for meeting life challenges," we can break the stereotypes that aging is an automatic period of decline.

Head and Heart

Each of us hopes, as a helping person, to engage our own best impulses, impulses from the heart. We hope to make the last years successful ones for our clients and for the older adults in our own families. This process, of course, requires some training, learning and, often, unlearning of stereotypes about aging. (See Worksheet 1.1 to explore our consciousness about older persons.) Again, our use of the sixth set of principles, "Older adults need to be meaningfully connected," and "Personal and social contexts affect learning," is central to our connections with older persons so that they do not become isolated or buy into debilitating stereotypes.

Learning Progression

Throughout life, learning can be our guarantor of competence in coping with the daily demands of living; learning can be our capital in contributing to others in our social network of family, friends, and associates; learning can be our energy invested in helping to influence and shape the flow of human events; learning can be our talent for expressing our inner selves; and learning can be our hope in transcending and illuminating our bounded human experience. In understanding the lives of older adults, learning can provide the means for making connections.

Yes, learning will accompany us throughout life in many and varied ways. We can count on an inherent capacity for learning as a lifelong resource with both manifest increases and some likely decreases in capacities. We can take charge progressively of our learning throughout life. Our needs can be met and our emotions can be managed as we pursue the challenges of growth and development. The fifth set of principles, "Continuity of self is lifelong," and "Life experience is the foundation and resource for all learning," expresses the deepest appreciation of the human capacity to meet the challenges of the last stage of life. We understand that our connections with each other are a central part of a dynamic process.

Part IV

Journey into the Future

Part IV distills key principles of gerontology and adult education and serves as a call to action to those prepared to address older adults' concerns about the quality of life and life satisfaction. It also discusses the imperative facing all who wish to be helpers—to connect successfully with older adults—whether as family members, friends, or as professionals. In order to foster the process of personal growth and development of a most precious resource, our elders, we must connect with one another as caregivers, making an effort to network, refer, cooperate, link, and cofacilitate. We must continue to learn about aging and understand that each of us is also on a path to our highest developmental potential. We look to older adults to inspire us: connecting is a mutual process of growth.

CHAPTER 7

Challenges for the Future

> Thank you for your lives.
> (An old world saying)
>
> Learning never ends.
> (U.S. postage stamp)

To connect with older adults, the touchstone for our future and our past, we have much to learn: patience, resiliency, survival. Our world has been in a period of change so profound, so rapid, and so pervasive that no other generation has faced the challenges of today's older population. Much of this change is attributable to technological developments. We have become one world in every aspect of daily life. While the technological component eases our survival, the human component is still necessary to enhance the quality of our lives. Human connections provide continuity, intergenerational strength, and courage. Having lived through numerous changes, disasters, and other challenges, older adults continue to hope, to love, and to care. "A human being," wrote C. J. Jung, "would certainly not grow to be seventy or eighty years old if this longevity had no meaning for the species to which he belongs" (1933, p. 109).

We have started on a journey in which older adults figure much more prominently in our society and culture than they have in the past. We have, in our desire to connect with them, found a grounding in both principles of aging and learning. We explored how to identify opportunities and employ strategies to help us connect along a continuum of needs. We have entered the lives of several individuals and engaged in reflection and dialogue. Now it is time to begin the journey into the future.

We shall introduce you to what we believe constitute the hallmarks of successful approaches and responses to meet the challenges of connecting with older adults. Finally, we invite you to share your experiences in making good connections happen. Send us examples of programs that address the social and developmental needs of older adults.

MAJOR CHALLENGES

To meet the needs of older adults in the 21st century, we must become more proficient in several key areas:

1. Making approaches
2. Learning responses
3. Building selves
4. Building others
5. Building bridges

Making Approaches

What is a "helping person" and how can one truly help? If you are working with older adults as a professional, paraprofessional, volunteer, adult educator, or family member, consider *how* to help and *when* to intervene. Responding to the challenges of present and future necessitates a clear sense of commitment, knowledge, and advocacy. Part III suggests possible strategies to be considered in various situations. The strategies selected depend on levels of need as discussed in Chapter 5: independent (no intervention needed); in need of assistance (help without intruding); and dependent (help without taking away dignity and independence).

In making true connections, we engage the head and heart. We are guided by emotion, loyalties, perceptions about aging—and often these feelings come from our earliest personal influences. In connecting with older adults, these caring impulses are essential: they give spirit to our work and guide our endeavors on behalf of older persons. However, we must also engage the head, the rational part of our consciousness, taking information at hand and locating it in a theoretical framework. This process requires an understanding of the dynamics of learning and, often, the unlearning of stereotypes about aging. Readers may review Part II, Foundations for Practice, in which a theoretical and empirical framework for connecting with older adults is developed (see Figure 4.1). Making connections requires a knowledge base as well as good intentions.

Learning Responses

One challenge of the future is educational. The demands for an educated work force and an educated citizenry in this increasingly complex world are escalating. In responding to this imperative, adult educators must understand how development occurs, what environments promote community, and how to optimize cognitive, physical, and psychosocial growth. Research and theory assist adult education practitioners in their work with family members, volunteers, pastoral workers, community organizers, home companions, geriatric workers, and elders themselves. Furthermore, knowledge of how older adults themselves learn, and what impact education can have on their lives is essential to our work.

This book has sought to increase awareness of what it means to age, how learning occurs, and what educational responses and approaches facilitate human growth in the last stage of life. Refer to Worksheet 2.1, where you placed yourself on the lifeline and made statements about the aging process. On the basis of what you have read, ask yourself: How have I changed? And how might I influence others to change their attitudes and understanding of aging?

One challenge is to become alert to incidents of *ageism*, the holding of these stereotypes about older adults. Stereotypes (or "myths of aging") include the beliefs that all older persons are senile, that they are fragile, that they are loving cookie-baking grannies, that they are cranky selfish old biddies, that they reside in nursing homes, that they are "unproductive" or incapable of learning. Robert Butler, who coined the term ageism, observed,

> We must begin by systematically analyzing the many myths and distortions about aging. Too much is attributed to age that is actually due to disease, disability, social adversity, personality, educational level, alcoholism, life-style, or the environment. (1990, p. 179)

Indeed, much of the disability associated with aging can be environmental. It is our job, as educators about aging and as practitioners, to focus on the developmental potential of mature people and to promote the view that working with older adults is an opportunity for reciprocal learning. We must inform others that older people are not all alike; nor do they resemble media or folkloric presentations.

Armed with knowledge and the zeal of educators, we must explore ways to create environments which maximize the capabilities of older adults. Aging offers an opportunity to find the greatest meaning in one's life.

Building Selves

We must build selves, build others, and build bridges. To build selves we must develop an ongoing awe and appreciation for the human community. Our first pair of principles, that "Aging is a developmental process" and that "Learning is a process involving multiple personal changes," creates a framework for adaptation and success. We know that each person has the ability to grow and that each learner has a "need to know and demand for change" specific to his or her developmental stage. These needs may extend from a trivial new behavior to a pervasive restructuring in attitudes, values, or sense of self. In seeking to connect, how might we provide support for others to name their own changes? Mrs. Schultz may ask for information on housing. Mr. Evans may wish cardiac fitness education. Each older adult is an individual with a personal history of meeting the need for change.

The second pair of principles, that "Each older adult is unique" and that "Individual needs, emotions and approaches to learning shape the learning experience," is important for building self. The task, again, is to explore the personal world of each older adult and to allow the individual to determine what path would be most helpful. Trust is essential in all that we do. Our earliest moments of life are entwined with trust, and our last moments alive are again dependent on trust. (Refer to Erikson's theory in Table 2.1.) Every moment of risk, of relationship, of growth, is connected with trust. In aging, again, we are reminded of the essential nature of trust: Do we trust our friends? children? health? medical and social helpers?

In making approaches or responding to elders' perceived changing status, we must present ourselves as available, appreciative of their competencies, and supportive of their autonomy. When we suggest interventions—a change of diet, medical attention, or an exercise regime—we will need to build a relationship. For example, the dietician who doesn't acknowledge Mrs. O'Leary's social and family context in planning a menu, will fail to help her make a change.

Building Others

In making connections with older persons, adult educators must remember that aging is a developmental process, one in which each stage of life plays a significant part (Wolf, 1992). Trust, a feature of our first developmental stage, is integrated at each level of maturity. We must rely on trust to implement the third pair of principles, "Older adults should maximize physiological and psychological capacities," and "Learning capacity is adequate for meeting life challenges," as many older adults may feel that aging has deprived them of their own capacity to participate in learning for safety, wellness, disease prevention, political advocacy, or retraining for the workforce. It is important to educate older adults themselves so that they do not develop an attitude that they are inadequate, or unteachable (as implied in, "You can't teach an old dog new tricks.") When Jim Rogers met with Mr. and Mrs. Denton, he asked them about their household maintenance. Clearly, the neighbors had expressed some concern over the rundown condition of the front yard. He was impressed, however, to find that Mrs. Denton had sent her hand mower out to be repaired and would be resuming her weekly lawn chores. "How," he asked, "can you do that yard all by yourself?" "I'm only 76, young man," she responded, "and have been studying judo on Saturdays. When the mower gets back this week, I'll see to the yard in no time."

The fourth pair of principles, that "Locus of control is a central issue throughout life" and "The learner actively constructs the future," connected in perspective. Each of us must take responsibility for conducting our lives, and, to some extent for making personal decisions. As caregivers, we must understand that building others is an investment in our own development. We must respect others' decisions even though we think we could "help" them by making decisions for them. Helen and Elizabeth Roland got a call from Mr. Collins' daughter-in-law. Mr. Collins, she said, was continuing to spend Sundays at the racetrack, despite a serious stroke the previous year. There was a concern, she said, with the 92-year-old's love of the races and of betting. "I pray for him every day," said Mr. Collins' daughter-in-law. However, what Helen and Elizabeth recalled from their course on gerontology was that locus of control—one's sense that he or she is in charge—is much more important than we think. Indeed, the cognitive workout of reading the race forms and handicapping horses was excellent for Mr. Collins. They wisely decided to back off, not to interfere with Mr. Collins' hobby.

Building Bridges

To build bridges, we must renew our own belief in the developmental potential of late life and recognize that there is no such thing as "them" and "us"—only "us." As one Rhode Island school child wrote about older adults:

> Older folks are
> Just older yous
> And older mes.

Each of us is an old person (some more fully unfolded than others) who craves to be connected and appreciated. What we want for ourselves is probably not any different from what older adults want: to continue to be connected and included.

The fifth pair of principles, "Continuity of self is lifelong," and "Life experience is the foundation and resource for all learning," confirms the individuality and personal growth potential for each learner, no matter what his or her age. The last pair of principles, that "Older adults need to be meaningfully connected" and that "Personal and social contexts affect learning," reaffirms that all people—regardless of age—belong to a community. Robert Butler has stated, "Another major intervention against ageism would be to mobilize the productive capabilities and contributions of older people. Society would be wise to develop incentives for part-time employment, entrepreneurism, and more extensive participation of older persons as volunteers" (1990, p. 179).

In building bridges, we must find ways to network, form coalitions, and link up with others who are working within our communities. We must connect with diverse individuals and families from different cultures, with different values. Those values which support collective interests and respect for self and other persons are sorely needed if we are to ensure a society today and in the future that is more diverse, more humane, more civilized, and more universally caring for its members. To function within and to work to perfect our world of which we are the inheritors demand that we commit ourselves to learning: that is one of the most fundamental manifestations of and requirements for "good citizenship." Edith Marshall spent two weeks learning about the world of Gretchen Hutchins. She found that Miss Hutchins volunteered in seven different locations. She rocked babies at the daycare, delivered groceries to shut-ins, called at the bingo matches, ironed for her sisters, made evening calls to neighbors, cashiered at the church gift shop, and was a foster grandmother. Edith, who had planned to offer assistance to Miss Hutchins, decided to offer transportation to the volunteer sites. Often she, too, joined Miss Hutchins in these activities.

CONCLUSION

In connecting with others we also touch our future and our past: we mark our days with a meaningful combination of development and learning. Older adults are ourselves, our own future. To fully appreciate aging, we must think about our *own* aging. We must celebrate the development potential of each person. As we know, life is a process of change, from the moment of birth to the moment of death. Each of us, if we are lucky, will live a full and long life. Each of us must die. It is what we do with our days that matters. In Barbara Myerhoff's excellent study of elderly Jews, *Number Our Days*, one older man observes:

> In old age, we got a chance to find out what a human being is, how we could be worthy of being human. You could find in yourself courage, and know you are vital. Then you're living on a different plane. (1979, p. 198)

How important it is for us to learn about that "special plane"—the developmental mandate of the human being—and to bring out the strengths and capacity to learn in *all members* of our community! We believe it is the central focus of our work in connecting with older adults.

BIBLIOGRAPHY

American Association of Retired Persons (AARP). (1987). *A profile of older Americans*. Washington: AARP.

Aslanian, C. B., & Brickell, H. M. (1980). *Americans in transition: Life changes as reasons for adult learning*. New York: College Entrance Examination Board.

Atchley, R. C. (1987). *Aging: Continuity and change* (2nd ed.). Belmont: Wadsworth.

Atchley, R. C. (1994). *Social forces and aging: An introduction to social gerontology* (7th ed.). Belmont: Wadsworth.

Ausman, L. M., & Russell, R. M. (1990). Nutrition and aging. In E. L. Schneider & J. W. Rowe (Eds.), *Handbook of the biology of aging* (3rd ed.) (pp. 384–406).

Ausubel, D. P. (1968). *Educational psychology: A cognitive view*. New York: Holt, Rinehart & Winston.

Baltes, P. B. (1993). The aging mind: Potential and limits. *The Gerontologist, 33* (5), 580–594.

Bandura, A. (1977). *Social learning theory*. Englewood Cliffs, NJ: Prentice-Hall.

Bandura, A. (1986). *Social foundations of thought and action*. Englewood Cliffs, NJ. Prentice-Hall.

Bass, S. (1993). *Productive aging*. Report to the Commonwealth Foundation, Boston.

Birren, J. E. & Deutchman, D. E. (1991). *Guiding autobiography groups for older adults: Exploring the fabric of life*. Baltimore: Johns Hopkins.

Brookfield, S. D. (1987). *Developing critical thinkers: Challenging adults to explore alternative ways of thinking and acting*. San Francisco: Jossey-Bass.

Brookfield, S. D. (1989). Facilitating adult learning. In S. B. Merriam & P. M. Cunningham (Eds.), *Handbook of adult and continuing education* (pp. 201–210). San Francisco: Jossey-Bass.

Bruner, J. S. (1973). *The relevance of education.* New York: W. W. Norton.

Butler, R. N. (1982a). Age-ism, another form of bigotry. In S. H. Zarit (Ed.), *Readings in aging and death: Contemporary perspectives* (2nd ed.) (pp. 185–188). New York: Harper & Row.

Butler, R. N. (1982b). Successful aging and the role of life review. In S. H. Zarit (Ed.), *Readings in aging and death: Contemporary perspectives* (2nd ed.) (pp. 20–26). New York: Harper & Row.

Butler, R. N. (1990). A disease called ageism. *Journal of the American Geriatrics Society, 38* (2), 178–180.

Butler, R. N., & Gleason, H. P. (Eds.). (1985). *Productive aging: Enhancing vitality in later life.* New York: Springer.

Candy, P. C. (1991). *Self-direction for lifelong learning: A comprehensive guide to theory and practice.* San Francisco: Jossey-Bass.

Cattell, R. B. (1963). Theory of fluid and crystallized intelligence: A critical approach. *Journal of Educational Psychology, 54*(1), 1–22.

Cavanaugh, J. C. (1993). *Adult development and aging* (2nd. Ed). Belmont, CA: Brooks/Cole Publishing Co.

Deobil, S. (1989). Physical fitness for retirees. *American Journal of Health Promotion*, 4(2), 85–90.

Dittmann-Kohli, F. & Baltes, P. B. (1990). Toward a neofuctionalist conception of adult intellectual development: Wisdom as a prototypical case of intellectual growth. In C. N. Alexander & E. J. Langer, (eds.), *Higher states of human development* (pp. 54–78). New York: Oxford University Press.

Erikson, E. (1963). *Childhood and society* (2nd ed.) New York: W. W. Norton.

Erikson, E. (1982). *The life cycle completed.* New York: W. W. Norton.

Erikson, E., Erikson, J. M., & Kivnick, H. Q. (1986). *Vital involvement in old age.* New York: W. W. Norton.

Feingold, E., & Werby, E. (1990). Supporting the independence of elderly residents through control over their environment. *Journal of Housing and the Elderly*, 6 (1–2), 25–32.

Fiske, M., & Chiriboga, D. A. (1990). *Change and continuity in adult life.* San Francisco: Jossey-Bass.

Gagne, R. M. (1970). *The conditions of learning* (2nd ed.). New York: Holt, Rinehart & Winston.

Gardner, H. (1983). *Frames of mind.* New York: Basic Books.

Goldberg, A. P., & Hagberg, J. M. (1990). Physical exercise in the elderly. In E. L. Schneider & J. W. Rowe (Eds.), *Handbook of the bi-*

ology of aging (3rd ed.) (pp. 407–428). New York: Van Nostrand Reinhold.

Guilford, J. P. (1967). *The nature of human intelligence.* New York: McGraw-Hill.

Hale, N. (1990). *The older worker: Effective strategies for management and human resource development.* San Francisco: Jossey-Bass.

Havighurst, R. J. (1972). *Developmental tasks and education* (3rd. ed.). New York: McKay.

Jarvis, P. (1992). *Paradoxes of learning: On becoming an individual in society.* San Francisco: Jossey-Bass.

Jung, C. G. (1933). W. S. Dell & C. F. Baynes (trans.), *Modern man in search of a soul.* New York: Harcourt Brace Jovanovich.

Kaminsky, M. (Ed.). (1984). *The uses of reminiscence, new ways of working with older adults.* New York: Haworth Press.

Kegan, R. (1982). *The evolving self.* Cambridge: Harvard University Press.

Kimmel, D. C. (1990). *Adulthood and aging: An interdisciplinary, developmental view* (3rd ed.). New York: John Wiley & Sons.

Knowles, M. S. (1973). *The adult learners: A neglected species.* Houston: Gulf.

Langer, E. J., & Rodin, J. (1977). The effects of choice and enhanced personal responsibility: A field experience in an institutional setting. *Journal of Personality and Social Psychology, 34*(2), 191–198.

Lewin, K. (1947). Frontiers in group dynamics: Concept, method and reality in social science. *Human Relations, 1*, 5–41.

Maddox, G. L. (Ed.) (1987). *The encyclopedia of aging.* New York: Springer.

Mahler, M. (1976). *The psychological birth of the human infant.* New York: Basic Books.

Maslow, A. H. (1970). *Motivation and personality* (2nd ed). New York: Harper & Row.

McClusky, H. Y. (1974). Education for aging: The scope of the field and perspectives for the future. In S. M. Grabowski & W. D. Mason (Eds.), *Learning for acting* (pp. 324–355). Washington, D.C.: Adult Education Association of the U.S.A.

McClusky, H. Y. (1990). The community of generations: A goal and a context for the education of persons in the later years. In R. H. Sherron & D. B. Lumsden (Eds.), *Introduction to educational gerontology* (3rd. ed.) (pp. 49–73). Washington: Hemisphere.

McCrae, R. R., & Costa, P. T. (1984). *Emerging lives, enduring dispositions: Personality in adulthood.* Boston: Little, Brown.

Merriam, A. B., & Caffarella, R. S. (1991). *Learning in adulthood: A comprehensive guide.* San Francisco: Jossey-Bass.

Messick, S. (1976). Personality consistencies in cognition and creativity. In S. Messick and Associates, *Individuality in learning: Implications of cognitive styles and creativity in human development* (pp. 4–22). San Francisco: Jossey-Bass.

Mezirow, J. (1991). *Transformative dimensions of adult learning.* San Francisco: Jossey-Bass.

Moody, H. R. (1988). *Abundance of life.* New York: Columbia University Press.

Moody, H. R. (1990). Education and the life cycle: A philosophy of aging. In R. H. Sherron & D. B. Lumsden (Eds.), *Introduction to educational gerontology* (3rd. ed.) (pp. 31–47). Washington: Hemisphere.

Myerhoff, B. (1979). *Number our days.* New York: E. P. Dutton.

National Center for Health Statistics. (1994). *Current Population Reports,* Series P-25 (949). Washington: U.S. Government Printing Office.

National Council on the Aging. (1991). *Retirement planning program.* Washington: National Council on the Aging.

Neugarten, B. L. (1979). Personality and the aging process. In S. H. Zarit (Ed.), *Readings in aging and death: Contemporary perspectives,* (pp. 72–77). New York: Harper & Row.

Neugarten, B. L. (1990, March 1). Keynote address, Annual Meeting of the Association for Gerontology in Higher Education, Kansas City, MO.

Neugarten, B. L., & Datan, N. (1974). The middle years. In S. Arieti (Ed.), *American handbook of psychiatry,* (2nd ed.) (vol. 1) (pp. 592–608). New York: Basic Books.

Neugarten, B. L., & Neugarten, D. A. (1986). Changing meaning of age in the aging society. In A. Pifer & L. Bronte (Eds.), *Our aging society: Paradox and promise* (pp. 33–51). New York: W. W. Norton.

Neugarten, B. L. et al. (Eds.) (1968). *Middle age and aging.* Chicago: University of Chicago.

Perlmutter, M., & Hall, E. (1992). *Adult development and aging* (2nd ed.). New York: John Wiley & Sons.

Proust, M. (1981). *Remembrance of things past.* New York: Random House.

Rodin, J. (September 1986). Aging and health: Effects of the sense of control. *Science, 233,* 1271–1276.

Rodin, J., & Langer, E. J. (1977). Long-term effects of a control-relevant intervention with the institutionalized aged. *Journal of Personality and Social Psychology, 35*, 897–902.

Rogers, C. R. (1983). *Freedom to learn for the 80's*. Columbus: Merrill.

Rowe, J. W. (1987). *Toward successful acting: A strategy for health promotion and disease prevention for older persons*. The Beverly Lecture on Gerontology and Geriatrics Education, No. 2. Washington: The Association for Gerontology in Higher Education.

Rowe, J. W., & Kahn, R. L. (1987, July 10). Human aging: Usual and successful. *Science, 237*, 143–149.

Schaie, K. W., & Willis, S. L. (1986). Can decline in adult intellectual functioning be reversed? *Developmental Psychology, 22*, 223–232.

Schaie, K. W., Willis, S. L., Hertzog, C., & Schulenberg, J. E. (1987). Effects of cognitive training on primary mental ability structure. *Psychology and Aging, 2*(3), 233–242.

Shea, G. F. (1991). *Managing older employees*. San Francisco: Jossey-Bass.

Skinner, B. F. (1968). *The technology of teaching*. New York: Meredith Corporation.

Spence, A. P. (1989). *Biology of human aging*. Englewood Cliffs: Prentice Hall.

Springer, D., & Brubaker, T. H. (1984). *Family caregivers and dependent elderly: Minimizing stress and maximizing independence*. Newbury Park, CA: Sage Publications, Inc.

Stern, D. N. (1985). *The interpersonal world of the infant*. New York: Basic Books.

Sternberg, R. J. (Ed.). (1990). *Wisdom: Its nature, origins, and development*. Cambridge: Cambridge University Press.

Stevens-Long, J. (1984). *Adult life: Developmental processes* (2nd ed.). Palo Alto: Mayfield.

Thorndike, E. L. (1931). *Human learning*. New York: Appleton-Century Crofts.

Tough, A. (1971). *The adult's learning projects: A fresh approach to theory and practice in adult learning*. Toronto: Ontario Institute for Studies in Education.

Tough, A. (1982). *Intentional changes: A fresh approach to helping people change*. Chicago: Follett.

U.S. Bureau of the Census. (1992). *Census and You*. Washington: U.S. Government Printing Office.

U.S. Department of Health and Human Services. (February 1994). *Monthly vital statistics report*, 42 (7).

U.S. Department of Health and Human Services. (May 1994). *Monthly vital statistics report,* 42 (12).

Wolf, M. A. (1990). The crisis of legacy: Life review interviews with elderly women religious. *Journal of Women & Aging,* 2(3), 67–79.

Wolf, M. A. (1992a). Older adults & reminiscence in the classroom. *Adult Learning 3* (8), 19–21.

Wolf, M. A. (1992b). Personal development through learning in later life. In L. A. Cavaliere & A. Sgroi (Eds.) *Learning for personal development* (pp. 73–84). New Directions for Adult and Continuing Education, no. 53. San Francisco: Jossey-Bass.

INDEX